District of Columbia v. Heller

v. Heller

The Right to Bear Arms Case

LANDMARK SUPREME COURT CASES  GOLD EDITION

Tom Streissguth

 Enslow Publishers, Inc.
40 Industrial Road
Box 398
Berkeley Heights, NJ 07922
USA

http://www.enslow.com

Library of Congress Cataloging-in-Publication Data

Streissguth, Thomas, 1958–
    District of Columbia v. Heller : the right to bear arms case / Tom Streissguth.
      p. cm. — (Landmark supreme court cases, gold edition)
    Includes bibliographical references and index.
    Summary: "A group of private gun-owners claimed new gun control laws passed by the District of Columbia violated their Second Amendment right to bear arms. This book examines the issues leading up to the case, the people involved in the case, and the present-day effects of the Court's decision"— Provided by publisher.
  ISBN 978-0-7660-3430-3
    1. Heller, Dick Anthony—Trials, litigation, etc.—Juvenile literature.
    2. Washington (D.C.).—Trials, litigation, etc.—Juvenile literature.
    3. Firearms—Law and legislation—Washington (D.C.)—Cases—Juvenile literature. 4. Gun control—Washington (D.C.)—Cases—Juvenile literature.
    5. United States. Constitution. 2nd Amendment—Cases—Juvenile literature.
    I. Title.
  KF229.H45S77 2010
  344.7305'3309753—dc22

                                   2009010108

Printed in the United States of America.

062010 Lake Book Manufacturing, Inc., Melrose Park, IL

10 9 8 7 6 5 4 3 2 1

To Our Readers: We have done our best to make sure all Internet Addresses in this book were active and appropriate when we went to press. However, the author and the publisher have no control over and assume no liability for the material available on those Internet sites or on other Web sites they may link to. Any comments or suggestions can be sent by e-mail to comments@enslow.com or to the address on the back cover.

♻ Enslow Publishers, Inc., is committed to printing our books on recycled paper. The paper in every book contains 10% to 30% post-consumer waste (PCW). The cover board on the outside of each book contains 100% PCW. Our goal is to do our part to help young people and the environment too!

Photo Credits: Air Force Senior Master Sgt. Mike Arellano/National Guard Image Gallery, p. 62; Associated Press, pp. 16, 18, 71, 75, 91, 96; Corel Corporation, p. 49; Enslow Publishers, Inc., p. 27; © Jackson Walker, The National Guard Image Gallery, p. 81; © Ken Riley, The National Guard Image Gallery, p. 52; Library of Congress, pp. 4, 46, 58; Mollie Isaacs, Collection of the Supreme Court of the United States, p. 85; Photos.com, p. 7; Shutterstock Images LLC, pp. 1, 22, 29, 34, 42; Steve Petteway, Collection of the Supreme Court of the United States, pp. 72, 87; U.S. National Archives and Records Administration, p. 31; Wikimedia Commons, p. 12.

Cover Photos: Associated Press.

Contents

Notorious rival gangsters Al Capone (pictured here) and George "Bugs" Moran wreaked havoc on the streets of Chicago in the 1920s and 30s with their bloody turf wars.

Introduction

On the cold morning of February 14, 1929— St. Valentine's Day—four men approached the front entrance of the SMC Cartage Company on Chicago's North Side. Underneath their topcoats, the men were carrying heavy machine guns. One of them had a sawed-off shotgun. They were professional hit men, hired by Chicago's top mobster, Al Capone, to carry out a killing.

The group burst into the garage, surprising seven men gathered there. Posing as police officers, the four intruders ordered the seven to stand against a whitewashed brick wall. Then they opened fire. The garage filled with a terrible, thundering noise.

The seven victims, all but one of whom belonged to the North Side's Bugs Moran gang, slumped to the floor. All of them were dead or dying. The killers walked calmly out of the garage, climbed into two automobiles, and drove away. Within minutes, the howling of a dog could be heard from within the garage. The animal had crawled under a car for safety. The sound quickly brought passersby to the scene of the St. Valentine's Day Massacre.[1]

Although there were witnesses to these events, the police never solved the murders. The following years brought a wave of bank robberies, more gangland slayings, and the deaths of innocent bystanders caught in the cross fire. Outraged by the bloody killings, the press and the public called for new laws to control gangsters and their deadly weapons. There were few laws on the books, and the federal government had never passed a gun-control law.

In 1934, Congress took action, passing the National Firearms Act (NFA). Anyone owning a sawed-off shotgun or a machine gun had to register the weapon with the Internal Revenue Service (IRS), a division of the Treasury Department. They had to pay a registration tax of two hundred dollars. They were then granted a license. If they wanted to sell the weapon, they would have to pay the tax again.[2]

Making a New Kind of Law

Congress picked these weapons because bank robbers and gangsters favored them. They gave the user a deadly advantage over local police forces, which used single-shot revolvers. A sawed-off shotgun was easy to conceal and move from place to place. It was an easy weapon to sneak into a bank (there were no metal detectors in

Sawed-off shotguns were easy to conceal , so they were popular with criminals. The National Firearms Act of 1934 imposed a tax on such weapons as sawed-off shotguns and machine guns to make them expensive to own.

the 1930s). Machine guns were a hazard to innocent bystanders. They sprayed dozens of bullets in a few seconds, over a wide range of fire.

Lawmakers believed something had to be done about these weapons. The National Firearms Act (NFA)was the result. It was the first federal law to control gun ownership. Since the Constitution had been ratified, Congress had never passed such a law. Lawmakers had always believed the Constitution did not grant Congress the power to regulate guns nationwide. Only individual states had that authority. By the Constition, powers not specifically delegated to Congress are reserved to the states.

During the Depression, however, the power of the federal government was expanding. The economic emergency inspired new federal laws. Still, the Second Amendment to the Constitution stood in the way of an outright ban on guns. To work around the amendment, lawmakers were relying on the constitutional power of the government to raise taxes and to regulate commerce between the states.

This applied to the NFA as well as many other laws. Congress passed the NFA not as a prohibition on guns but as a measure to raise revenue (the registration tax) for the federal government. In this view, making it expensive to own a weapon would limit the use of these weapons by criminals.

The Case of Jack Miller

Over the next few years, the Treasury Department and the FBI used the NFA to chase down bank robbers and gangsters. On April 18, 1938, in Siloam Springs, Arkansas, treasury agents arrested Jack Miller and Frank Layton. They were small-time moonshiners, who made and sold illegal liquor (often at night, by the light of the moon). Miller and Layton were traveling between Oklahoma and Arkansas at the time. By the law, they were taking part in "interstate commerce."

The agents searched the car and confiscated a twelve-gauge Stevens shotgun, which had its barrel sawed off. Miller and Layton did not have a license for the weapon.

The federal government charged them with transporting an untaxed, federally controlled weapon across state lines.

The case went to the U.S. District Court in Fort Smith, Arkansas, where Judge Heartsill Ragon presided. Although Miller and Layton tried to plead guilty, Ragon refused to allow the plea. Instead, he appointed a defense lawyer for Miller and Layton.[3] The lawyer, Paul E. Gutensohn, argued that the NFA was a violation of the Second Amendment to the U.S. Constitution, which reads: "A well regulated militia, being necessary to the security of a free state, the right of the people to keep and bear arms shall not be infringed."[4]

Not only was the NFA unconstitutional, Gutensohn argued, but only states had the power to levy taxes on goods and services. (The federal government already collected taxes on income.) By collecting taxes on guns, the federal government was exceeding its authority.

Judge Ragon agreed and threw out the case. The federal government then made a second charge against Miller and Layton for transporting an *unregistered* gun across state lines. Ragon again acquitted Miller and Layton of violating the NFA. The lawyers representing the federal government appealed the decision to the Supreme Court, the highest court in the land.

United States v. Miller

The justices of the Supreme Court heard the case of *United States v. Miller* on March 30, 1939. Lawyers for the federal government appeared before the court to make their case. Gutensohn, who had earned no money from his work on the case, decided not to spend the time and money necessary to prepare himself and travel to Washington to appear at the hearing.[5] Layton had been dismissed from the case. (Soon after the hearing, Miller was shot and killed by a person or persons unknown near Chelsea, Oklahoma.)

Unopposed, the government lawyers made their argument supporting the NFA. Their first point was that the Treasury Department had the authority to collect revenue authorized by Congress. Second, the sawed-off shotgun in the possession of Jack Miller was not a "militia" weapon. Miller did not belong to an organized state militia, nor had he ever served in the military. Therefore, the Second Amendment did not protect his right to own the weapon.

The decision in *United States v. Miller* came down on May 15, 1939. The justices agreed with the government's position. They voted unanimously to overturn the trial court decision. The written opinion in the case stated: "In the absence of any evidence tending to show that possession or use of a shotgun having a barrel of less than eighteen inches in length at this time has some reasonable relationship to the preservation or efficiency of a well regulated militia, we cannot say that the Second Amendment guarantees the right to keep and bear such an instrument. Certainly it is not within judicial notice that this weapon is any part of the ordinary military equipment or that its use could contribute to the common defense."[6]

What the U.S. Constitution meant by "militia" was very important to the *Miller* decision. Also important were the precise meanings of "people," "well regulated," and "bear arms." These phrases, originally penned by James Madison, were key to every challenge to gun laws that followed, including the *District of Columbia v. Heller* decision that the Court would make in 2008.

Like many Supreme Court decisions, the *Miller* case raised more questions that it answered. To this day, people on both sides of the gun-control debate use it to support their arguments. Gun-control advocates, who believe laws restricting gun ownership are constitutional, believe the *Miller* decision supports a specific interpretation of "militia." Only the members of militias, organized to fight for the common defense, have a constitutional right to bear arms.

Those opposing restrictive gun laws believe the opinion means that gun ownership, in general, is constitutionally protected. They also believe the decision was partially in error. The justices of the Supreme Court did not realize that short-barreled shotguns were a common military weapon. In fact, such weapons *had* been in use by regular armies as well as militia. The government lawyers, of course, did not point this out. Because there were no lawyers arguing the other side, the justices were not fully informed. Thus the *Miller* case does not resolve the debate over gun control, nor does it set a precedent for further laws restricting gun ownership.

After handing down the opinion, the Supreme Court justices "remanded" (returned) the case to the district

James Madison (1751–1836) was the fourth president of the United States, serving two terms from 1809 to 1817. He is known as the "Father of the Constitution" because he wrote most of it.

court. The lower court would, it was hoped, examine the facts again, hear both sides, and make a different decision. But soon afterward, Jack Miller was killed. Frank Layton went to jail after agreeing to plead guilty in the criminal case. This plea closed all proceedings in the matter.

The modern gun-control debate has its origins in the *Miller* decision and the fact that the Supreme Court of 1939 did not spell out exactly what the Second Amendment permitted. Did a private citizen still have the right to own a gun for self-defense of the home? Did the government have the right to restrict an entire class of weapons, either by levying taxes or banning them altogether? Through the next seven decades, the Supreme Court would offer no opinion on these questions, until the case of *District of Columbia v. Heller*.

Trouble in the District of Columbia

CHAPTER 1

The case of *United States v. Miller* was a "landmark" Supreme Court case. For many years, lower courts used the case to guide their decisions. Meanwhile, the federal government continued to regulate certain weapons. The government relied on *United States v. Miller* as its authority.

Crime and gun violence worsened in the 1960s. This spurred stricter federal laws on firearms. In 1968, Congress passed the Gun Control Act. Instead of controlling large weapons, this law focused on small ones: "Saturday Night Specials." These cheap handguns were used in many robberies and murders. They were easy to buy and to hide. To end their legal sale, the Gun Control Act set down a minimum size for handguns.[1]

Gun violence worsened anyway. Crime rates soared in the inner cities, including Washington, D.C. The District of Columbia is the home of the federal government and the nation's capital city. In neighborhoods not far from the Supreme Court and the U.S. Capitol building, shootings were a common occurrence. The city's murder rate was one of the highest in the country.

In 1981, John Hinckley attempted to kill President Ronald Reagan with a handgun. The attack took place on a Washington, D.C., sidewalk, just outside a hotel where the president was making an appearance. Hinckley wounded Reagan and two other men, including Reagan's press secretary, Jim Brady. A bullet struck Brady in the head, paralyzing him.

The near assassination inspired a drive for new laws to register and to control the use of guns. In 1993, Congress passed the Brady Handgun Violence Prevention Act, also known as the Brady Bill. Anyone wanting to buy a gun had to wait five days and submit to a background check. Those convicted of a felony crime or having a record of mental illness or violence in the home were banned from buying a gun.[2]

The new laws did not resolve the debate over the Second Amendment to the Constitution. Sarah Brady, the wife of Jim Brady, supported new laws on guns. She became chairman of Handgun Control, Inc. This group had organized in 1974 to fight for passage of strict gun laws. The organization is now known as the Brady Campaign to Prevent Gun Violence.

The Brady Campaign gives its stand on its Web site: "Guns don't fall from the sky into the hands of criminals. The crime gun market is fed by a small, identifiable

Former press secretary Jim Brady holds a model of a gun trigger lock during a 1997 news conference in Washington. His wife, Sarah Brady (right), is chairperson of the Brady Campaign to Prevent Gun Violence. The organization sponsored the news conference to demand that laws be passed requiring child safety locks on all guns.

group of reckless gun dealers. We must stop the flood of illegal guns at its source: corrupt gun dealers who put profit ahead of public safety."[3]

Those opposing new gun laws saw them as an infringement of basic rights of U.S. citizenship. They also believed gun laws did not deter crime. As an example, they pointed to Washington, D.C., which had passed the strictest handgun law in the nation.

This side organized as well. Alan Gottlieb started

the Second Amendment Foundation in the same year as Handgun Control. On its Web site, the foundation quotes the Second Amendment to the Constitution and states: "The Second Amendment Foundation (SAF) is dedicated to promoting a better understanding about our Constitutional heritage to privately own and possess firearms."[4]

One other group overshadows all the rest in the gun-control debate: the National Rifle Association (NRA). This group began in 1871, just a few years after the end of the Civil War. It now has more than 4 million members. The NRA is one of the largest and strongest lobbying organizations in the country. It fights against the passage of gun-control laws in Congress and by the states and cities.

Opponents believe the NRA achieves its goals by threatening and intimidating lawmakers. Yet the NRA failed to stop the D.C. gun ban, as well as the Gun Control Act, the Brady Bill, and many other federal and local gun-control laws. Instead of new laws, the NRA believes existing laws should be better enforced. The organization supports bans on gun ownership by convicted felons and by the mentally ill.

Many other organizations work exclusively on the gun-control debate. They issue press releases, hold conferences, and send members to debate the opposition in the media. When an important court case begins, they file briefs with the court to give their side of the argument. Their leaders know that even the important

The National Rifle Association held its 138th Annual Meetings and Exhibits in Phoenix, Arizona, on May 15, 2009. The organization lobbies to protect the rights of gun owners.

decision in the case of *District of Columbia v. Heller* would not end the debate.

The D.C. Difference

The District of Columbia was founded as a special, independent zone for the federal government. It is not a state. The founding fathers wanted to prevent any conflict between the federal government and a state that might have authority over where the federal government operated. Therefore, the District of Columbia had no government of its own. It had no representation in

Congress, as each of the states did. It had no governor, mayor, or city council. Instead, Congress governed it directly. The District of Columbia was, and still is, largely governed by federal laws passed by Congress.

D.C. residents often protested against their lack of representation. They called for "home rule," meaning local elections for a mayor and council, and more say in how their city operated. Congress responded in 1973, passing a law that set up a city council for the District of Columbia. The office of D.C. mayor was also established. For the first time, elected leaders could pass ordinances for the city.

One of the most serious problems the new D.C. leaders faced was the high crime rate. Home rule did not make the streets of the city any safer. It did not make the D.C. police force more effective or reduce drug dealing or gang violence. Because most of the murders within the District of Columbia were committed with handguns, the city council took aim at their possession.

In 1976, the council passed the Firearms Control Regulation Act. This ordinance banned handguns, as well as semiautomatic and automatic weapons, from the District of Columbia entirely. Only police officers or security guards, while on the job, could carry one. Private citizens had to register handguns they already owned. The guns had to be securely stored away. If D.C. residents bought a handgun after the law was passed, they could not register it. "Long guns"—meaning rifles and shotguns—had to be kept unloaded. Long-gun owners had to take their guns apart or keep them locked with a trigger guard, which prevents the gun from firing. For violating the law, gun owners could be fined or jailed, or both.

The mayor and the council believed their law would be the first of many similar laws. They hoped that Maryland and Virginia, states that neighbor Washington, D.C., would also pass handgun bans. Very few cities and no states, however, passed complete bans on handguns. The D.C. ban remained the strictest in the nation. One exception was Chicago, the scene of the St. Valentine's Day Massacre. In 1982, the city passed a similar ban that is still in effect.

The New Crime Epidemic

For a few years, the District of Columbia saw a steady or falling murder rate. In 1976, the year the gun ban went into effect, there were 188 murders in the city. In 1985, there were 147.[5]

Yet crime in the city remained high. In one well-known case, intruders attacked three women in their home and kept them prisoner for fourteen hours. The police failed to respond to several 911 emergency calls. The case led to a lawsuit in federal court. The decision, in *Warren v. United States,* stated that the police had no legal obligation to protect private citizens. Those opposing the D.C. gun ban often mentioned the *Warren* case to support their stand: Private citizens have a constitutional right to own guns for self-defense.[6] A complete ban on handguns, in this view, violates this right.

In the early 1980s, meanwhile, a new form of cocaine

was spreading through the cities of the eastern United States. "Crack" was a purified form of cocaine that could be smoked. It was easy to make, very addictive, and, unlike regular cocaine powder, relatively cheap. Drug dealers had first made and sold crack in Miami, Florida. From that city, an epidemic of crack addiction spread north and soon reached the District of Columbia.

Crack dealing on the streets brought about more turf wars among drug dealers. Using cheap handguns, they fought over the right to sell in certain streets and neighborhoods. The police were ineffective in reducing crime. Several neighborhoods became open-air drug markets. Residents left their homes only when necessary. Some kept guns in their homes in defiance of the handgun ban. These guns were still legally for sale in the neighboring states of Maryland and Virginia.

The ban on handguns did nothing to deter the violence, and the murder rate rose once again. It reached 434 in 1989, 472 in 1990, 482 in 1991 (the all-time high), 443 in 1992, and 454 in 1993. Through the late 1990s and the first years of the twenty-first century, the murder rate fell again.[7] The crack epidemic began to abate. Among the urban young and poor, the drug went out of style, replaced by "softer" drugs, such as marijuana. Although crack dealing continued, it no longer caused murderous turf wars on the District of Columbia's streets.

Nevertheless, the gun ban did not seem to be doing much to keep the violence and murder under control. Gunfire became such a common sound in the city that

Despite the handgun ban, the murder rate in Washington, D.C., rose in the 1990s due to turf wars among drug dealers. Handguns were still legal and fairly easy to obtain in Maryland and Virginia.

the police deployed sensors on rooftops in the most violent neighborhoods. The sensors served as automatic 911 emergency calls. They picked up the sound of shots being fired and immediately directed the police to the scene of the shooting.

In the meantime, anyone living in D.C. who needed or wanted a gun had no trouble getting one. The buyer had to leave the District of Columbia to shop in Maryland and Virginia. Licensed gun dealers in these states were happy to sell anyone weapons. There were no laws demanding they identify their buyers or preventing a gun sale to a D.C. resident. One *Newsweek* reporter told the tale in a December 2007 article:

> Damon Sams doesn't spend much time worrying about restrictions on his right to bear arms. Now 19, the former drug dealer got his first gun, a .380 pistol, at 13, when he started selling marijuana and later crack on a street corner in Southeast Washington. "I wanted people to respect me and be scared of me," he says. He also wanted protection. As a kid, he'd seen his father shot dead in the street. He's been shot himself on two separate occasions. . . . The gun ban was never a concern when Sams went looking for a new weapon. He'd just call up friends in Maryland who would get him anything he wanted. "I know people with a gun license," he says casually. "You just throw them a couple hundreds."[8]

While the District of Columbia struggled with street violence and drug dealing, many law-abiding people were keeping weapons in their homes, illegally, to protect themselves. There seemed to be a fundamental conflict between the law and the actions of ordinary citizens. Sooner or later, a court challenge to such a law usually takes place. Lawyers stand ready to write briefs (legal essays) making their points and to argue at a public court hearing. If they believe a law is unconstitutional, they may organize a "test case" that will eventually reach the Supreme Court for a final decision.

District of Columbia v. Heller

The Supreme Court was established by Article III, Section 1 of the Constitution and was first organized in 1790.[9] It decides the most important questions of the law, interprets the Constitution, and applies that document to the laws and actions of federal, state, and local governments. If the Supreme Court finds a law unconstitutional, it can strike down that law. The police and the courts will no longer be able to enforce it.

The District of Columbia's handgun ban was one such law that came under Supreme Court review in the fall of 2007. The decision of the nine justices would affect not just the District but all other cities that had passed similar handgun bans. It would also decide the fundamental meaning of the Second Amendment.

The Road to the Supreme Court

CHAPTER

2

For four years during the 1990s, Clark Neily worked as a "first chair" or lead trial lawyer in Dallas, Texas. While other attorneys and assistants prepared the case, Neily spoke for his clients and made their cases in front of a judge and jury. The job demanded a complete mastery of the details of each case. It also demanded a gift for public speaking, debate, and persuasion.

In 2000, Neily joined the Institute for Justice in Washington, D.C. The members of this law firm held to the libertarian view: a strict interpretation of the Constitution and limited government power. They saw government power steadily expanding in the modern era. This expansion of federal laws and authority, to libertarians, threatens the freedoms guaranteed by the original founding fathers of the nation.

The Institute for Justice found plaintiffs with cases bearing on these issues. Their clients were confronting the government on a wide range of issues—taxes, free speech, and the conduct of their businesses. They brought their cases to court to argue their points and, hopefully, win decisions in their favor.

Neily and his colleagues believed firmly in their cause. They were not merely "hired guns" working to help their paying customers. On its Web site, the Institute for Justice still promotes Neily with these words: "If there were a black belt in litigation, Clark Neily would own one. This is one hard-charging, take-no-prisoners, lay-it-on-the-line kind of guy."[1]

Along with public-interest law firms, several "think tanks" in Washington argue over important points of law, economics, and social issues. The members of these nonprofit organizations write research papers, editorials, and books. They organize forums and conferences, at which members and guests debate the issues.

Edward Crane, a national chairman of the Libertarian Party, founded the Cato Institute in 1977. He named this nonprofit after "Cato's Letters," a series of pamphlets written by two Englishmen in the early eighteenth century, well before the Revolutionary War. The Cato Letters argued for an end to the tyranny and arbitrary rule of kings.

Following the principles of Cato's Letters, the Cato Institute proclaims on its home page: "The mission of the Cato Institute is to increase the understanding of public policies based on the principles of limited government, free markets, individual liberty, and peace."[2] The Cato Institute attracted scholars and writers who

King George III ruled Britain at the time of the Revolutionary War. The American colonists fought for a government free from kings.

agreed with its founding principles. Robert Levy joined the organization in 1997 as a "senior fellow" in the study of the Constitution. Levy also joined the Institute for Justice.

Levy's political outlook, and his views on modern law and government, were very similar to those of Clark Neily. In Levy's view, the Supreme Court was going badly astray in its interpretations of the Constitution. He was a firm believer in staying strictly within the letter of the document. The Court should not create new constitutional rights, such as the right to privacy found in the case of *Roe v. Wade*, to legalize abortion. Nor should the Court infringe on basic rights guaranteed by the founding documents. These included a constitutional right of qualified citizens to bear arms of their choosing. In the view of Levy and Neily, both of whom lived in the District of Columbia, the D.C. gun ban clearly violated this right.

In 2000, Neily contacted Levy to discuss the Second Amendment and the Supreme Court. The two agreed that too much time and too many laws had passed since *United States v. Miller.* For too long, the Second Amendment had been the subject of debate and disagreement. The two sides on the gun-control debate could not agree on the meaning of "militia," the power of Congress to regulate guns, or the constitutional right of private citizens to bear arms. What exactly did the Second Amendment mean for gun laws and gun ownership? The country needed another decision on the Second Amendment that would resolve the issue.

Neily and Levy decided to build a test case. Their goal was to challenge and to eventually defeat handgun bans on constitutional grounds by bringing a case to the Supreme Court. If they lost in federal court, they would appeal the decision to the Supreme Court. If they won in federal court, they hoped the opposing side would appeal.

The Court of Final Appeal

The Supreme Court interprets the Constitution to decide the most important questions of law. The Supreme Court has the authority to strike down a state or federal law—such as a handgun ban—on constitutional grounds. If the justices decide against a law, this allows a direct challenge to similar laws in other states or jurisdictions.

But thousands of cases are appealed to the Supreme Court every year. The Court does not have the time to hear every appeal. Only a select few cases touch on important constitutional questions. For a review to take place, a party to a case in a federal appeals court must file a petition for a writ of certiorari. This is a formal

The Supreme Court has the authority to strike down a state or federal law if the Court believes the law violates the Constitution. Those supporting gun ownership hoped this would be the case with the D.C. handgun ban.

request for the Supreme Court to hear the case and to make a decision on it.

When the Supreme Court grants the writ, the case is scheduled for a hearing. Lawyers for both sides present their arguments before the nine justices, who can ask questions and debate the case, and the Constitution, with the attorneys and among themselves. A decision, in the form of a written opinion, can take several months to be published after the hearing.

To pull together their test case, Levy and Neily gathered a team of attorneys and scholars, including Alan

Gura and Gene Healy. Both men researched Second Amendment cases in state and federal courts. They examined the decisions of the Supreme Court. Levy also began searching for a client. He needed someone, unconnected with the Cato Institute, to bring a complaint to the courts.

There was one tough problem standing in their way: the Fourteenth Amendment to the Constitution, which states in part, "[N]or shall any State deprive any person of life, liberty, or property, without due process of law."[3]

Does the Second Amendment apply to the states according to this "due process" doctrine? This important question prevented any clear interpretation. Taking the Fourteenth Amendment into account, the Supreme Court may not give a clear ruling on the Second. If the Second Amendment does not apply to the states, then there would be no opportunity to challenge state gun laws on a constitutional basis.

There was one way to go around the question of "due process" and the power of states to make and to enforce their own gun laws. Levy began searching for a client living not in a state, but in the District of Columbia.

Finding Plaintiffs

Levy's search for plaintiffs to file the case took several months. Finally, the team selected six people who had agreed to sign their names to the complaint and to stand through a trial. The case of *Parker v. District of Columbia* was filed on February 10, 2003.

The original handwritten first page of the Fourteenth Amendment from the National Archives. One interpretation of the Fourteenth Amendment defended a state's right to make and to enforce its own gun laws as long as it was done with "due process."

One of the plaintiffs was Shelly Parker. She was forty-four years old and worked as a software engineer. She lived in a neighborhood not far from the U.S. Capitol building. Although it was near the heart of the federal government, Capitol Hill could be a dangerous place for people who actually lived there. Drug dealers stood on street corners, selling their goods to passersby and to buyers who drove through in their cars. Arguments over territory and money led to frequent gun battles in the streets.

Parker did not move out of the neighborhood or take shelter in her home. Angered by the crimes, she confronted the criminals. She patrolled her street alone and called the police when she suspected criminal activity. Her defiance brought danger. Vandals damaged her car and her property. In broad daylight, people shouted threats while standing just outside her home. For Shelly Parker, keeping a gun for self-defense seemed like a good idea.

Plaintiff Richard Heller

Richard Heller worked as a security guard at the Thurgood Marshall Federal Judiciary Building. His employer, a private security company, supplied guards to public and private buildings. Heller was trained and licensed to carry weapons on the job and to use them if necessary. But the D.C. gun ban prevented him from keeping his service weapon at home, for his own defense. Every day, before leaving for home in the Capitol

Hill neighborhood, he had to turn in his weapon and ammunition.

Heller had strong opinions about the role of government. He opposed gun laws and saw them as a sign of a tyrannical government trying to take away the natural rights of its citizens. He was not shy about expressing these views. A *Newsweek* article quoted him as saying, "I can protect [federal workers], but at the end of the day they say, 'Turn in your gun, you can't protect your home.'"[4]

Through a mutual friend named Dane von Breichenruchardt, Heller met Robert Levy. Von Breichenruchardt was president of the Bill of Rights Foundation. When he realized that Heller was going to be part of a test case on the Second Amendment, he gave Heller some advice: apply for a permit for his handgun (which Heller kept stored outside the District of Columbia). Von Breichenruchardt knew that D.C. would turn down the application. He also knew the appeals court would dismiss Heller from the case if Heller did not suffer a legally recognized injury, meaning a denial of his permit.

Heller followed this advice, which eventually made him the sole plaintiff in the Supreme Court case. But Heller's strong opinions posed a problem for the lawyers working on his behalf. Heller did not make a very sympathetic figure, at least for a federal judge. He was neither meek nor defenseless. Levy and his partners advised Heller to keep his strong opinions to himself, at least until the case was decided.

In the meantime, Levy himself freely spoke to the press about the *Parker* case. He supported an effort in

Gun ban opponents argue that forbidding law-abiding citizens to own guns makes them vulnerable to violent attacks from intruders who may otherwise be scared off.

the fall of 2004 by some members of Congress to pass a law striking down the D.C. ban. While the law worked its way through a debate in Congress, Levy told editor John Fund at the *Wall Street Journal* that "[r]ight now, if someone breaks into a poor person's home here, their only choice is to call 911 and pray the police arrive in time. . . . That's not good enough, and let's hope members of Congress grant the right to bear arms to people who can't afford to live in the safe neighborhoods they go home to at night."[5]

Opposition from the NRA

Meanwhile, the case drew no support from the National Rifle Association. The NRA, which supported individual rights to gun ownership, believed it likely that the Supreme Court would uphold the D.C. gun ban. The organization thought it best to wait until the court had more justices sympathetic to its views. If the Supreme Court decided to uphold the gun ban, then a strict interpretation of the Second Amendment would prevail. This would result in more limits on gun ownership, perhaps for a very long time.

Also, the NRA had its own lawsuit working through the court system. This was *Seegars v. Ashcroft*. This suit was filed in the federal court in April 2003, soon after the Parker case. This case involved five plaintiffs who lived in high-crime areas of Washington, D.C., and who owned, or sought to own, long guns and/or handguns for self-defense. Sandra Seegars, the lead plaintiff in the case, was a member of the District of Columbia

Taxicab Commission and sought to own a pistol for defense of her home. NRA lawyers challenged not only the District of Columbia but also the federal Department of Justice, which was now under the leadership of John Ashcroft, a staunch supporter of individual gun rights. They filed the case after Robert Levy and Clark Neily filed the *Parker* case. With the *Seegars* case, the NRA brought its own plea for Second Amendment rights to the Supreme Court.

The NRA wanted to use its case as the basis for the first Supreme Court decision on the Second Amendment since the case of *United States v. Miller*. After filing the suit, the NRA attempted to consolidate the two cases. This would combine them so that a single decision could be rendered. In effect, this would take the case out of Robert Levy's hands. Fortunately for Levy and the *Parker* case, the motion to consolidate was denied.

Case Dismissed!

Unfortunately for the NRA, there was a fundamental problem with the *Seegars* case. In early 2004, the district court ruled that the plaintiffs in the case did not have standing to bring a lawsuit. The plaintiffs had brought a "preenforcement" challenge—one that takes place even before the law in question is enforced against them. And such a challenge, unless there is a threat of imminent prosecution, must be dismissed: "In this case, the plaintiffs have suffered no injury as a result of the District of Columbia's proscriptive gun control statutes. First, they are unable to point to any 'credible threat of imminent prosecution.' . . . [C]ase law is clear and unequivocal that for a plaintiff to have standing to pursue a preenforcement challenge outside of the First Amendment context, the threat of prosecution must be imminent."[6]

The lawyers for the plaintiffs appealed this decision to a federal appeals court. Then, in March, the court dismissed the *Parker* lawsuit brought by Robert Levy. As planned, Levy appealed his decision as well. His case was stayed (meaning temporarily halted) so that the *Seegars* appeal could be decided first. In February 2005, the *Seegars* appeal was denied.

The *Parker* case resumed. The three appeals court judges handed down an important decision in March 2007. Five of the plaintiffs were found to be without standing to challenge the D.C. gun ban. Their applications for gun permits had not been denied, and they did not face an imminent, real threat of prosecution under an unconstitutional law—instead, their claim was only theoretical. They could be prosecuted and punished for *breaking* the law. But theoretical injury by an unjust law was not enough for the appeals court to declare the law unconstitutional.

Richard Heller survived as a plaintiff in the case. He had attempted to register one of his handguns, a pistol that he knew was banned within the District of Columbia. The license had been denied, as Heller knew it would be. Thus, he had suffered a clear "injury" through the workings of the law. He alone had standing to challenge it.

The District of Columbia claimed it had the right to

deny Heller his license. If Heller wanted a weapon, he could buy a legal rifle or shotgun, get a permit for it, and store it according to the city ordinance.

In *Parker v. District of Columbia,* the appeals court disagreed. By a 2–1 decision striking down the ban, the court found that handguns are "arms" as mentioned in the Second Amendment and that the Constitution protects the right to bear arms whether or not a citizen is an active participant in a militia. This was the first decision by a federal appeals court to strike down a gun law on Second Amendment grounds.

The dissenting judge on the appeals court panel wrote that the District of Columbia, not being a state, cannot possibly have a state militia and therefore the right expressed in the Second Amendment does not apply within the city.

According to the majority opinion, however, the Second Amendment means every individual citizen has a right to bear arms. Gun owners do not need to be part of a militia, and the guns they own do not have to be used in a military conflict. The justices remanded the case to the district court with instructions to reverse its decision. Heller and Levy had won their case—but they were not yet at the doors of the Supreme Court.

The District of Columba obliged Levy and Heller by petitioning for a rehearing (the winning party in a case cannot appeal the decision to a higher court). This plea was denied by the appeals court. The city then petitioned the Supreme Court for a hearing. The Supreme

Court granted the petition and scheduled a review of the case of *District of Columbia v. Heller*.

In the meantime, the NRA—having lost its case—was supporting a new federal law to combat the D.C. ban. Levy disagreed with this "legislative" strategy. In his view, laws could always be challenged, struck down, changed, or ignored. They could be passed in some cities and states, and not in others. The whole patchwork quilt of gun laws across the nation, which often conflicted with federal laws, lay at the heart of the endless gun law debate. Instead of new laws, he wanted a Supreme Court decision that would find any and all outright gun bans unconstitutional.

The NRA-sponsored law failed to pass. The way was clear for Levy and Heller to appear before the Supreme Court. In the meantime, President George Bush had appointed two new members of the Supreme Court. Justice Samuel Alito and Chief Justice John Roberts were known as "conservative" justices, who supported a strict interpretation of the letter of the Constitution. They also were known to agree with the "individual rights" view of the Second Amendment.

The NRA at this point threw its support to their case. Lawyers for the organization wrote an amicus curiae ("friend of the court") brief, or written argument about the facts of the case and the relevant law that should be involved in the final decision. An amicus brief is presented by someone who is not a party to the case, in order to support one side or the other with his or her own point of view and legal reasoning.

The NRA's brief opposed the D.C. gun ban and supported Richard Heller. Vice President Dick Cheney, an ardent supporter of gun rights, endorsed the brief, as did several members of Congress. At the same time, gun-control advocates were busy sending their own amicus briefs to the court. The case of *District of Columbia v. Heller* became a battleground of conflicting ideas on the Second Amendment. The essence of the fight was a different view of the nation's early history and how and why, exactly, the amendment had been written.

The Context of the Constitution

CHAPTER

3

English settlers began arriving in North America in the early seventeenth century. These colonists were escaping oppressive government in England. The English monarchy enforced strict laws on their religious beliefs and conduct.

The settlers established several new colonies, including Massachusetts and Virginia. In the meantime, their homeland was suffering political turmoil. In 1688, the English population, largely Protestant, rebelled against James II, the Catholic king of England. A member of the Stuart dynasty, James had controlled the people with a "standing" army under the command of Irish Catholic officers. His soldiers had disarmed Protestants, making any challenge to his authority impossible.

The overthrow of James II had an important result: the authority to make the laws of the land passed to the Parliament, a body of elected representatives. William and Mary, the new

A modern re-creation of the Mayflower. Pilgrims set sail on the original Mayflower from England in 1620, hoping to find freedom in America.

Protestant rulers, passed a Declaration of Rights in the spring of 1689. Parliament passed its own version, the Bill of Rights, in December. Article VII provided that "[t]he subjects which are Protestant may have Armies for their defence Suitable to their Condition and as allowed by Law."[1]

By this new right, Protestants could now arm themselves, if necessary, for defense against tyranny. The members of Parliament also hoped that the right recognized by Article VII would prevent a restoration of the Catholic Church as the official church of England. However, the right to form armies was still subject to law and to regulation by Parliament.

The Bill of Rights enshrined a fundamental principle of English government: Parliament was supreme, and the king must rule by its laws. But the individual ownership of weapons, in England and elsewhere in Europe, still depended largely on a person's standing in society. Members of the aristocracy were permitted weapons for the purposes of hunting and for defending their estates against criminals. But to prevent illegal poaching in the countryside, as well as rebellion in the cities, the lower orders were not allowed free access to weapons, especially firearms. Owning a gun was an offense punishable, in some realms, by death.

Trouble on the Frontier

In the middle of the eighteenth century, the British colonies were thriving along the eastern coast of North America. To the west, in the Appalachian Mountains, the British were battling the French for control of a lucrative trade in furs and for the right to claim land for settlement. A war erupted on the colonial frontier in the 1750s. The French allied with American Indian tribes living in the forests and mountains of the Appalachian region.

By the 1760s, the British had prevailed. The French retreated to the Great Lakes region and north to Canada. The British colonies continued to grow with new settlers. The British government levied taxes on the colonists to help pay for the defense of their colonial possessions.

The colonies organized militias to defend frontier towns against American Indian raids. The militias were made up of all able-bodied men in each community. They used their own pistols and muskets or drew weapons from a central armory.

As they were responsible, largely, for their own defense, the colonists came to resent British taxation. They had no representation in the British parliament and no say in their own governments, which were led by British-appointed governors. The British troops stationed in their homes and cities seemed more an army of occupation than a defense force.

In his 1983 article "Handgun Prohibition and the Original Meaning of the Second Amendment," author Don B. Kates describes the colonial militias:

> Even if they had wanted a standing army, the colonists were unable either to afford the cost or to free up the necessary manpower. Instead, they adopted the ancient practice that was still

in vogue in England, the militia system. The "militia" was the entire adult male citizenry, who were not simply allowed to keep their own arms, but affirmatively required to do so. . . . With arms readily available in their homes, Englishmen were theoretically prepared at all times to chase down felons in response to the hue and cry, or to assemble together as an impromptu army in case of foreign invasion of their shire.[2]

Guns v. Snowballs

On the evening of March 5, 1770, a crowd gathered in front of the Customs House in the troubled city of Boston, the largest port in the Massachusetts colony. The people were growing angry and resentful at the occupation by the British troops. Several members of the crowd began throwing snowballs at the "redcoats." One colonist came forward and struck a British sentry with a club. The order rang out: "Fire!" A volley of British musket bullets killed three men instantly. Two more later died of their wounds.

News of the Boston Massacre spread quickly through the city. A wave of rebellion swept through the Massachusetts colony. To the colonists, the posting of British troops in the colonies was no protection against the French or the American Indians. Instead, it was a hindrance and a threat. The one-sided confrontation, between men armed with real weapons and men armed with wooden clubs and snowballs, represented the

An engraving of the Boston Massacre. The angry colonists were armed only with snowballs and wooden clubs, no match for the British soldiers and their guns.

unjust treatment of the colonists by the tyrannical British monarchy.

Over the next few years, the British army took steps to disarm the colonists. British troops raided public arsenals and seized weapons, and they banned their possession in several cities. They staged raids in private homes, searching for guns. On a spring day in 1775, in Lexington, Massachusetts, one of these raids took place while a local militia was drilling on the village green. The confrontation led to a running firefight between the militiamen and British troops—the first shots of the Revolutionary War. On July 6, two colonial leaders, Thomas Jefferson and John Dickinson, wrote the Declaration of Causes of Taking Up Arms. The document gave the reasons for the rebellion, describing one of many complaints as follows:

> The inhabitants of Boston being confined within that town by the general their governor, and having, in order to procure their dismission, entered into a treaty with him, it was stipulated that the said inhabitants having deposited their arms with their own magistrate, should have liberty to depart, taking with them their other effects. They accordingly delivered up their arms, but in open violation of honour, in defiance of the obligation of treaties . . . the governor ordered the arms . . . to be seized by a body of soldiers; detained the greatest part of the inhabitants in the town, and compelled the few who were permitted to retire, to leave their most valuable effects behind.[3]

Acts such as these, with the British troops raiding armories and disarming the colonists, only inspired more support for the growing rebellion. In 1776, the Continental Congress, made up of colonists' representatives, passed the Declaration of Independence and proclaimed the founding of the United States of America.

In the meantime, Virginia passed a Bill of Rights that stated, in part, that "a well regulated Militia, composed of the Body of the People, trained to Arms, is the proper, natural, and safe Defense of a free State" and that "standing Armies, in Time of Peace, should be avoided, as dangerous to Liberty."[4] In its constitution, Pennsylvania granted its citizens the "right to bear arms" for the purpose of self-defense, as did assemblies in North Carolina, Maryland, Delaware, Vermont, and Massachusetts.

All these early constitutions had passages related to standing armies. In the view of the colonists, the presence of the British troops had become a threat to individual liberties. Such armies could only exist if the people were disarmed. This robbed an individual of his natural right to defend himself and his property. Thus, standing armies were a violation of natural rights and at all times to be avoided. Citizen militias, on the other hand, were a guarantee of liberty. A militia would serve to protect the interests of the people. Moreover, a militia of volunteers organized for defense was not likely to infringe on the rights of outsiders.

Writing a Constitution

The colonists defeated the British army, declared their independence, and established the United States of America. This new nation was a republic (a state without a monarch), in which lawmakers and a president were elected by a vote of adult male (and free) citizens.

In the meantime, eight states passed declarations of their own. These documents set out the basic rights of their citizens. The individual right of a private citizen to own weapons was not among them. "What appear

This famous 1817 painting by John Trumbull is often identified as depicting the signing of the Declaration of Independence. In fact, it actually shows the drafting committee presenting its work to the Congress.

instead," writes legal scholar Carl Bogus, in a brief for the Supreme Court, "are statements . . . affirming the virtue of a well-regulated militia, the danger of standing armies, and the importance of maintaining civilian control over the military."[5]

To set down the basic framework of the government, James Madison and several other leaders wrote a national constitution. As former English colonists, they relied on English law and tradition, including the 1689 Bill of Rights, in creating this document.

Two factions were strongly at odds over the wording of the Constitution. The Anti-Federalists sought power for the individual states and to prevent the federal (national) government from becoming another version of the tyrannical English monarchy. The Federalists wanted to concentrate more power in the federal government. They believed this would prevent the new country from becoming a loose collection of states, with no common interests or national unity.

The Anti-Federalists believed that the Constitution, as it was written, would not protect individual liberties. Thus, certain amendments would also be necessary to guarantee those liberties. One such right would be the right to free speech and expression. Another would be freedom to practice the religion of one's choice. This, it would hoped, would prevent the violent struggle between Protestant and Catholic faiths that had brought centuries of trouble to England.

Another amendment should guarantee the right of the people to form militias and to bear arms. This would prevent the use of standing armies by the government to control the population.

Who Controls the Militia?

The framers of the Constitution did not debate the right of individuals to bear arms. They believed this should be left up to the states, which would have the authority to pass laws governing personal property, including guns.

Instead, the framers debated the militias: how to organize them and how to command them. During the Revolutionary War, the militias had turned in a mixed performance. Some were poorly trained and armed. Their members had little notion of keeping formation, firing in ranks, or defending positions. They had trouble with military discipline and the hardships of long-distance marching.

As a result of this history, many believed the national government should set down uniform rules for the militias. The Federalists wanted control of the militias by the national government. James Madison, among others, sought "uniformity" in regulating the militias. Eventually, the matter was turned over to a committee. This group wrote a report and created Article I, Section 8, granting Congress the power to "provide for organizing, arming, and disciplining the Militia, and for governing such Part of them as may be employed in the Service of the United States, reserving to the States respectively, the Appointment of the Officers, and the Authority of training the Militia according to the discipline prescribed by Congress."[6]

This meant Congress had the power to arm the militia, with weapons it saw fit for the purpose. Congress would set down rules about the kind of weapons the militia would use. Congress had the authority to control how these arms were furnished, either by the states or the federal government. The states were responsible for appointing officers and training militia members.

So like many other parts of the Constitution, the militia clause was a compromise between Federalists

American militiamen wait patiently as the British Army approaches. The Battle of Bunker Hill took place on June 17, 1775, in Boston, Massachusetts, and although the colonists lost the battle, they showed the British that they were a force to be reckoned with.

and Anti-Federalists. The federal government and the states would share responsibility and authority over militias.

For many years after the adoption of the Constitution, the United States would have no national army. It was hoped that the state militias would take care of defense on the frontier. To make them effective, however, one more constitutional right would be necessary: the right of the people to bear arms.

The Pennsylvania Difference

The first ten amendments to the Constitution were known as the Bill of Rights. The name was taken from England's 1689 Bill of Rights. James Madison was the author of the Bill of Rights and of the Second Amendment, guaranteeing the right of citizens to bear arms. Congress voted on and approved the Bill of Rights in 1789.

Each state held a convention to debate the Constitution and to vote on ratifying it. Ratification was a condition of statehood. But the framers believed that all thirteen colonies must become states. Therefore, if the states rejected any part of the Constitution, the framers would have to reject that part or to rewrite it.

Nevertheless, the debates over ratification could be long and difficult. Many states did propose changes to the Constitution to better fit their ideas of what fundamental rights of citizens should be.

Pennsylvania, like the other states, held a convention to argue the points of the national constitution. This colony had suffered a bloody frontier history. It had also gone through violent civil strife between its settlers and its governors. The two sides could not agree on the proper authority of the governor. In addition, the Quakers who had settled Pennsylvania had strong religious beliefs against taking up arms and fighting wars.

As a result, Pennsylvania had not formed a militia of its own. Frontier villages were on their own in defending against Indian attack and the British army. During the Revolutionary War, Pennsylvania colonists had petitioned their governor to force adult males to take up arms and to join militia units.

This history had an effect at the constitutional convention in Pennsylvania. Several delegates proposed this change to the Second Amendment: "[T]he people have a right to bear arms for the defense of themselves and their own state, or the United States, or for the purpose of killing game, and no law shall be passed for disarming the people or any of them, unless for crimes committed, or real danger of public injury from individuals."[7]

The framers of the Constitution rejected this change. Pennsylvania eventually ratified the Constitution and the Second Amendment as James Madison wrote it. The language of the Pennsylvania convention still has an effect on the modern gun debate, however. Those favoring gun rights quote it to show that people of colonial times understood "bear arms" to mean an individual right, not necessarily depending on militia service.

Those favoring gun-control laws point out the historical context: Pennsylvania had a dire need for militia service from its citizens for self-defense on the frontier and during the Revolution. They also believe it shows the reasonable regulation of firearms was accepted practice, even as the new country was debating its Constitution.

Guns on the Frontier

In the early nineteenth century, a national armory was storing weapons in Springfield, Massachusetts. From Springfield and the Connecticut River valley, a gun industry supplied weapons for the American army and for settlers heading west to the frontier. These settlers needed rifles for hunting and for defense of their homes. After Samuel Colt invented the revolver, a small and easy-to-conceal weapon, handguns also became commonplace.

Concealed weapons, however, were subject to state laws and city ordinances. In Tennessee, one resident was arrested for carrying a concealed bowie knife. In 1840, the case arrived at the Tennessee Supreme Court. In its decision, the court examined the meaning of the state constitution, which stated: "[T]he free white men of this State have a right to keep and bear arms for their common defense" and also that "no citizen of this state shall be compelled to bear arms provided he will pay an equivalent, to be ascertained by law." In other words, in Tennessee, the "right to bear arms" was directly linked with required military service.

Nevertheless, an individual's right to own guns for the defense of his own home never came into question. Through the nineteenth century, a long gun was a common article in frontier homes. Such a weapon was often in use, either for hunting or for self-defense. Only after the frontier was closed and the United States became a largely urban society did the courts begin to debate the meaning of the Second Amendment.

The Original Intent: Individual v. Collective Rights

CHAPTER

4

The modern gun-control debate boils down to one very basic question over the meaning of the Second Amendment. Does this sentence guarantee each individual a right to bear arms, or does it only confer a collective right, one that the people have as long as they belong to an organized militia?

Historians, justices, lawyers, and politicians have argued for many years over this point. The decision in *District of Columbia v. Heller* may resolve it. Even if a constitutional right is generally agreed on, however, the gun debate will continue.

Presser v. Illinois

Before *United States v. Miller,* two major decisions by the Supreme Court touched on the meaning of the Second Amendment. In the case of *United States v. Cruikshank,* decided on March 27, 1876, the Supreme Court had

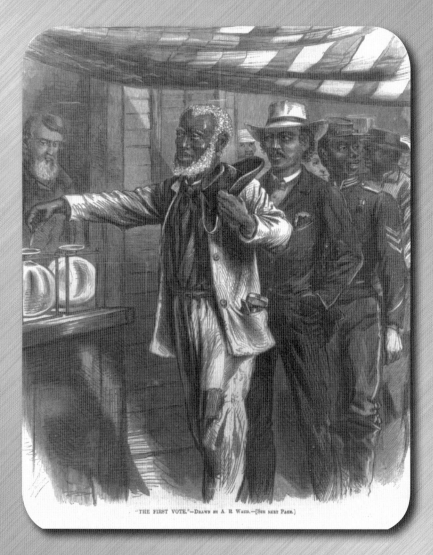

"THE FIRST VOTE."—Drawn by A. R. Waud.—[See next Page.]

The Fourteenth Amendment made former slaves citizens of the United States. Therefore, African Americans should have had the same rights as white citizens, including the right to vote and bear arms. However, many Southern states were passing unfair laws to strip African Americans of their rights.

to decide on how the Fourteenth Amendment and the Bill of Rights should be applied to the actions of state governments. In the aftermath of the Civil War, many Southern states were passing laws restricting the rights of newly freed blacks, including the right to bear arms.

The case of *United States v. Cruikshank* arose from a bloody street battle between black freedmen and a militia made up of armed white citizens in Colfax, Louisiana. In the aftermath, several members of the militia were indicted under the Enforcement Act of 1870, which made it a federal crime to deprive any person of his constitutional rights.

In its decision, the Supreme Court overturned the indictments. The court found that the Second Amendment affects federal, not state, government and laws. In addition, the Bill of Rights does not confer rights on the citizens—it only restricts the action of governments. Since it was made, the *Cruikshank* decision has prompted many legal scholars to conclude that the Second Amendment allows the states to restrict guns as they wish and does not confer the right of an individual to own a gun.

In 1886, the amendment as well as the meaning of "militia" came under Supreme Court scrutiny. In the years after the Civil War, the city of Chicago was growing rapidly. As a railroad center, Chicago made a good location for companies in the business of making or moving goods. People flooded into the city from the eastern United States and from Europe, eager for well-paid work. But labor troubles also plagued Chicago. There were frequent strikes and all-out riots between workers and armed men working for their bosses. Many private companies organized large armed gangs to deal with any trouble on the factory floor.

One young worker, a German American named Herman Presser, joined the Instruct and Defend Association. The members organized—and armed—large groups of like-minded workers to fight against the company gangs.

The group held military drills in public spaces in Chicago. Presser led one such drill in September 1879. In the eyes of the law, Presser and his mates were taking part in an illegal action. They had no authorization from the state to organize a private military company. They were not part of any state-controlled militia, nor did they have a license to parade. The police arrested Presser and charged him with forming an illegal militia. He pleaded not guilty, was found guilty by a court, and was sentenced to a fine of ten dollars.

The case of *Presser v. Illinois* eventually reached the Supreme Court. Herman Presser cited the Second Amendment and his constitutional right to form a militia. The Supreme Court disagreed. States could ban militias, if they so chose. Although Presser had a constitutional right to assemble and to associate with whomever he wished, he did not have a right to form a private military company or to drill that company with arms. Furthermore (as also decided in *Cruikshank*), the Second Amendment was a limit on Congress and its federal laws, not on that of the states. Therefore, the state of

Illinois had the authority to ban private militias and to charge those who organized them with a violation of its laws.

The *Presser* decision resolved for a time the question of gun laws and their constitutionality. It gave states and cities the authority they needed, should they so choose, to limit the ability of citizens to form private armed militias and—by extension—their right to bear arms. This authority had its limits, however. States and cities could not entirely ban weapons for use by private citizens, as that would prevent these same governments from calling up militias, should they need to do so. According to the *Presser* opinion: "It is undoubtedly true that all citizens capable of bearing arms constitute the reserved military force or reserve militia of the United States as well as of the States. . . . [T]he States cannot . . . prohibit the people from keeping and bearing arms, so as to deprive the United States of their rightful resource for maintaining the public security, and disable the people from performing their duty to the general government."[1]

The *Presser* decision established that the Second Amendment applied to federal law, which governed the District of Columbia. For this reason, the city would become, more than a century later, the testing ground for another important decision on the basic meaning of the amendment.

The Meaning of Collective Rights

The militia of colonial times exists today in a very different form. Each state can summon National Guard units in

Members of the Texas National Guard distribute food, water, and ice in Cleveland, Texas, October 5, 2005, after Hurricane Rita tore through the area.

case of military emergency or natural disaster. Members of the National Guard are volunteers. They commit some of their time to training for such events. National Guard units have also been sent overseas, and several are taking part in the occupation of Iraq.

In colonial times, militia members used their private firearms while carrying out militia service. But the arms used by modern National Guard units are supplied by the federal government. Those who favor "collective rights" point this out in support of their argument. Times, and warfare, have changed since the

Revolutionary War. The guarantee of a right of private individuals to bear arms is no longer relevant, as modern "militia" units do not use private weapons.

The collective rights position also puts a specific meaning on the word "people" as the Second Amendment uses it. "People" in this amendment means the states, as the representatives and defenders of their citizens. The "people," in the form of the individual state, has the right to bear arms, in the form of a militia. Also, Article I, Section 8, of the Constitution provides Congress with the power to arm the militia. The authority devolves to the states and their militias, not to individual citizens.

Those favoring collective rights also believe that Congress and the states have the legal authority to regulate firearms. After all, the Second Amendment does begin with "A *well-regulated* militia . . ." If a state or city sees a need to regulate weapons, it can do so, just as it can control who can drive a car or operate a business.

Even a complete ban on a certain class of weapons, such as a handgun (or a tank), is within the legal power of a city, such as Washington, D.C. The city council may seek to improve public safety as it sees fit. In this view, the requirement that legal arms in the home must be unloaded and carry a trigger lock is also reasonable.

The Meaning of Individual Rights

Those disagreeing with collective rights see "the people" in the Second Amendment as meaning each and every citizen. They support this view by pointing out the use of "people" in other parts of the Constitution, specifically the First Amendment and the Fourteenth Amendment. In both these amendments, the courts have long held that the rights belong to individuals. In addition, the word "rights" in the Second Amendment, as in other parts of the Constitution, means the "rights" of individuals. At no point in the document does the government enjoy "rights." Instead, it has "powers" or "authority."

Scholar Don Kates points out the position of this side succinctly in his article "Handgun Prohibition and the Original Meaning of the Second Amendment":

> [To deny that "people" means individual citizens] the following set of propositions must be accepted: (1) when the first Congress drafted the Bill of Rights it used "right of the people" in the first amendment to denote a right of individuals (assembly); (2) then, some sixteen words later, it used the same phrase in the second amendment to denote a right belonging exclusively to the states; (3) but then, forty-six words later, the fourth amendment's "right of the people" had reverted to its normal individual right meaning; (4) "right of the people" was again used in the natural sense in the ninth amendment; and (5) finally, in the tenth amendment the first Congress specifically distinguished "the states" from "the people," although it had failed to do so in the second amendment.[2]

A federal appeals court supported the individual rights model in the case of *United States v. Emerson,* decided in 2001. In this case, the respondent, Timothy

Emerson, had been found in violation of a federal law, which prohibits anyone under a restraining order from owning a weapon. Emerson claimed the law violated his Second Amendment rights. The appeals court agreed, stating that "[t]he plain meaning of the right of the people to keep arms is that it is an individual, rather than a collective, right and is not limited to keeping arms while engaged in active military service or as a member of a select militia such as the National Guard."[3]

This decision had a wide-ranging effect. The attorney general of the United States, John Ashcroft, wrote a memorandum to all U.S. attorneys who prosecute cases on behalf of the federal government. The memo stated that the court "undertook a scholarly and comprehensive review of the pertinent legal materials and specifically affirmed that the Second Amendment 'protects the right of *individuals*, including those not then actually a member of any militia or engaged in active military service or training, to privately possess and bear their own firearms.'"[4]

The Bill of Rights often comes into play when the Supreme Court decides important cases. The meaning of its amendments is not always clear, especially when applied to modern society. Although the First Amendment guarantees a right to free speech, does it also allow citizens to make violent threats or to advocate acts of terrorism? The Supreme Court has decided many First Amendment cases in the past, and the precise meaning of "free speech" is constantly being debated and decided anew.

The Constitution has been the subject of study and debate ever since it was written. The modern view of the Constitution falls into two general camps: those who favor a flexible interpretation of the Constitution and those who favor a very strict interpretation. The flexible, "liberal" camp, in general, sees the Bill of Rights as recognizing a wider range of natural rights than expressly mentioned in the original document. "Conservatives" see these rights as limited to just what James Madison mentioned, and no more. They favor "strict constructionists" as justices to the Supreme Court.

In the case of the Second Amendment, however, the stances are different. Political "liberals" favor a strict interpretation of the Second Amendment, believing it only recognizes a *collective right* to bear arms by, very specifically, militia members. A more flexible interpretation of the amendment persuades gun-rights supporters, who are generally conservative, to see an *individual right* to bear arms for all citizens (who by the traditional definition of "militia" belong to the state militias). In practice, this means they oppose new gun-control laws and seek to strike down restrictive laws that are already on the books.

Supporters of the individual-rights model believe that scholars of history and the Constitution are on their side. They point out that their view of the amendment has come to be known as the "Standard Model." They also quote from history books, in particular the words of Tench Coxe, a Pennsylvanian who wrote a commentary on the Bill of Rights in 1789, which states: "As civil rulers, not having their duty to the people duly before them, may attempt to tyrannize, and as the military forces which must be occasionally raised to defend our country, might pervert their power to the injury of their fellow citizens, the people are confirmed by the next article in their right to keep and bear *their private arms.*"[5]

Soon after the publication of this article, James Madison, the author of the Second Amendment, wrote a letter to Coxe agreeing with his view. But Madison may still have had organized militias in mind when writing the Second Amendment. The true meaning, and context, of the amendment is still up for debate, more than two hundred years after Madison set it to parchment.

The Politics
of a Decision

CHAPTER

5

The Supreme Court stands majestically on First
Street, NE, just across the street from the
U.S. Capitol building. It resembles a Greek
temple, with slender columns rising at the top
of a sweeping staircase. Inside, the building is
hushed, with floors and walls of beautifully
polished granite and marble. It seems very far
from the troubled streets of the Capitol Hill
district, just to the east, where Richard Heller
made his home. It also seems very far from
the rough-and-tumble world of politics and
presidential campaigns.

But the Court works with politics very much
in mind. In the view of the public, Supreme
Court decisions are political "victories"
or "defeats." Presidents appoint Supreme
Court justices, and the U.S. Senate confirms
them. The justices serve for life, although
they can retire. When a justice leaves the
Court, the president must decide on another

appointment. He or she will make that decision based on the candidate's views of the law and the Constitution. The next election will also play a role.

Politicians running for office state their views on whom should be appointed and whom should not. Some voters consider their stand very carefully before casting their ballots. Certain questions of law decided by the Supreme Court have shaped modern American society. Other questions have not yet been resolved, and a future Supreme Court may have to decide them.

Gun Rights and Party Politics

In 1994, Congress passed a sweeping ban on "assault weapons." The law classified machine guns and some kinds of semiautomatic guns as assault weapons. It became illegal to buy, to sell, or to possess an entire class of weapons. The law was challenged on constitutional grounds in dozens of cases brought to lower courts all over the country. In every case, the ban—whether a federal ban or a similar state ban—was upheld, or an appeals court refused to review a lower-court decision.[1] In New Jersey, a group known as the Coalition of New Jersey Sportsmen challenged the law as being vague and unconstitutional. The Third Circuit Court of Appeals upheld the state ban, and in November 2001, the Supreme Court refused to hear the case.

Nevertheless, the assault-weapons ban came under heavy fire. Gun-rights supporters believed it violated the Second Amendment. They voiced their criticism of the law. Then they took their opinions to the voting booth.

The NRA sent out millions of letters to its members, reminding them of who had supported the law. The organization urged its members to vote against lawmakers who disagreed with its position.

In the same year the law passed, the Democratic Party suffered a defeat in congressional elections. Members of the party had written, passed, and supported the assault-weapons ban. The Republican Party scored important gains, and it won a majority in Congress. Many people believe the assault-weapons ban played an important role in the Republican victory.

The backlash continued, even as the Democratic president Bill Clinton won re-election in 1996. Then, in 1999, two students at Columbine High School in Jefferson County, Colorado, went on a rampage with handguns, sawed-off shotguns, and explosive devices. As minors, they had bought their weapons illegally. The shooting left twelve students and a teacher dead; both of the perpetrators committed suicide. The Columbine massacre led to a national outcry over lax gun-control laws.

In 2000, Republican George W. Bush, a gun-rights supporter, defeated Democrat Al Gore for the presidency. The Republicans again won control of the Congress. This result meant that the next Supreme Court justices would likely be supported by Republicans. In the meantime, the assault-weapons ban was allowed to lapse in 2004, ten years after its passage.

There had been no new appointments to the Supreme Court since 1994. Through Bush's first term as president, there were no changes on the Court. Bush was reelected in 2004. He finally had a chance to make a Supreme Court appointment in 2005, when Justice Sandra Day O'Connor announced she would retire.

O'Connor represented a "swing vote" among the nine justices. Although she had been a Republican in public political life, she was not necessarily conservative on judicial matters and the Constitution. Republicans and

Protesters demonstrate against the National Rifle Association's annual meeting taking place in Denver, Colorado, less than two weeks after the April 20, 1999, shooting in Columbine High School. The public demanded that more be done to make access to guns impossible for youths and disturbed individuals.

gun-rights supporters believed the new justice might replace her "swing vote" with one more reliably conservative.

Bush appointed John Roberts to replace O'Connor. Before the Senate could vote on Roberts's appointment, however, Chief Justice William Rehnquist died. The president then withdrew the nomination of Roberts as the successor to O'Connor and nominated Roberts to succeed Rehnquist as chief justice. Controlled by Republicans, the Senate supported Bush in his appointment of the conservative Roberts to the court. The president then announced that White House counsel Harriet Miers would take the seat vacated by O'Connor.

Miers faced strong opposition, especially among political allies of George Bush. Miers was Bush's personal attorney. She did not have any experience as a judge. Her views on gun control and the Second Amendment were not clear. Her opponents accused Bush of simply nominating a personal friend for the job, one who was not qualified to be a Supreme Court justice.

When opposition to Miers continued to grow, Miers asked Bush to withdraw the nomination. Bush agreed and then appointed Samuel Alito to the

Conservative John Roberts became chief justice after the death of William Rehnquist.

Supreme Court. Alito was a conservative justice who sat on the Third Circuit Court of Appeals. He had supported the Bush administration in several cases brought to his court. He had also written a minority opinion in 1996, disagreeing with the two other appeals-court judges who had decided that Congress had the authority to ban machine guns. "Earth to Sammy—who needs legal machine guns?" stated Jim Brady, for whom the Brady Bill was named. "The Chicago mobsters of the 1930s would be giddy. But the man I worked for [President Reagan], who gave us Sandra Day O'Connor and signed the 1986 machine gun ban, would be shaking his head."[2]

Alito had "strict constructionist" views on the Constitution. Conservatives favor strict constructionists as justices who will stick to the letter and original intent of the Constitution. Alito had also written more than three hundred opinions as an appeals court judge. It was fairly clear that he favored an individual-rights view on the constitutional right to bear arms. Conservatives and Republicans favored his appointment. Democrats and liberals opposed him.

The nomination process included hearings before the Senate Judiciary Committee. The senators did not raise the issue of the Second Amendment. They did question Alito on his position on illegal wiretapping of private U.S. citizens. In his opinions, Alito had supported the authority of the Justice Department and the FBI to carry out such wiretapping. This prompted Senator Patrick Leahy, a Democrat from Vermont, to write: "This is a nomination that I fear threatens the fundamental rights and liberties of all Americans now and for generations to come. This President is in the midst of a radical re-alignment of the powers of the government and its intrusiveness into the private lives of Americans. This nomination is part of that plan."[3]

The Judiciary Committee held a vote on Alito, which resulted in a 10–8 recommendation to the Senate for his confirmation. The Republicans on the committee all voted in support of Alito. The Democrats all voted against him.

After the Judiciary Committee hearings and vote, the Senate voted to confirm Alito as the next Supreme Court justice. The nominations of Roberts and Alito, replacing Rehnquist and O'Connor, now provided a more conservative Supreme Court. The attorneys for Richard Heller realized their chances of a favorable decision, if the case ever reached the Supreme Court, were improving.

Meanwhile, More Gun Laws

As the case of *District of Columbia v. Heller* worked its way through the court system, many states were passing new gun laws. These laws were banning the possession of firearms by convicted criminals or the mentally ill.

Lawmakers do not want to see their laws struck down by the courts. They are careful to word legislation in order to avoid a legal challenge. For this reason, supporters of the new laws claimed they were dealing with a law enforcement issue and not attempting to decide anyone's constitutional rights. The laws did not limit ownership of weapons by the people *in general*. They only affected specific classes of people, those who in their view should not own weapons.

In an attempt to go around the Second Amendment topic of "arms," several states passed new laws dealing only with ammunition. California passed a law requiring that ammunition carry microscopic imprints. If the ammunition were ever used in a crime, police could use these imprints to help trace the gun owner and the place where he or she bought the gun. Several other states followed California's example.

Lawmakers in favor of more access to guns were also hard at work. A new law in Florida allowed citizens

A candle is lit at midnight on April 16, 2009, in remembrance of the thirty-two victims of the Virginia Tech shootings two years earlier.

to carry concealed weapons. Florida and other states passed laws allowing workers, and customers, to bring weapons to a place of employment, as long as they had a concealed weapons permit and kept the guns in their cars. Other laws allowed students and teachers the right to carry weapons on college campuses. This law was a response to a murderous rampage that took place at Virginia Tech University on April 16, 2007, when a lone gunman killed thirty-two people before killing himself. The gunman, Seung-Hui Cho, had purchased one semi-automatic pistol online and another at a gun shop in Roanoke, Virginia. He passed the background checks required of all gun purchasers, although he concealed the fact that he had been treated for mental illness. He had also legally bought ammunition on eBay.

The states also were passing laws in an attempt to trace guns that are lost or stolen. Several states now require gun owners to make a report to the police whenever this happens. Other laws require anyone buying ammunition to go through a background check.

The background system itself, known as the National Instant Criminal Background Check System, was the subject of a new federal law passed in early 2007. The law granted money to the states that improved the information put into the system. The system now includes mental health as well as criminal records. This allows gun dealers a way to prevent the mentally ill as well as criminals from getting weapons.

For lawmakers in some states, the new laws posed a problem. In Pennsylvania, for example, the legislature defeated a new law on reporting stolen or lost weapons. Although the law did not pass, the state had not even debated a gun law for more than fifteen years. Pennsylvania's constitution specifically grants individual citizens the right to own guns, and traditionally that right is never questioned or challenged. Kate Harper, one representative who voted for the law, told the *New York Times*: "These are difficult votes for me because it hurts me with my caucus, and it also hurts with really strong Republican voters who don't want government interference. . . . On the other hand, I've got soccer moms and people who have never fired a gun and are afraid of them."[4]

The Florida concealed-carry law was the subject of an intense debate. It was opposed by the Florida Chamber of Commerce, which filed a lawsuit to overturn it. The debate continued even after the Supreme Court handed down its decision in *District of Columbia v. Heller*. One employee of the Disney company, which runs amusement parks in central Florida, decided to challenge the company's complete ban on concealed weapons (even by employees who keep the weapons in their cars). In July 2008, Edwin Sotomayor, who worked at Disney's Animal Kingdom theme park in Orlando, brought a .45-caliber pistol to work, keeping it locked in his trunk. Security guards found his gun, and the company immediately fired him.

The company argued that it had the right to ban weapons by customers or employees in the interest of preventing any terrorist acts on its property. It also claimed that because fireworks were stored at its theme parks, it should be exempt from the law, which specifically exempts companies that have explosives on their property.

Sotomayor claimed he needed the gun to deter any violent acts against him while he was driving to and from work. The NRA quickly weighed in on the case. A spokesman named Marion Hammer said, "It's typical of Disney. . . . They have no regard for the safety of their customers or their employees."[5]

The Disney Company eventually changed its gun policy. Employees would be allowed to bring guns to work. They had to keep the weapons locked in their cars. The owners had to have concealed weapons permits. The guns could not be visible, and they could not be taken out of the car at any time while the employees were at work.

The compromise was one of thousands that businesses were making all over the country over the right to have a concealed weapon. To avoid an expensive court case, companies bent strict rules on guns to the letter and the spirit of the law. Yet the spirit of the Second Amendment, even after *District of Columbia v. Heller*, continues to be a subject for debate.

The Court Decides

Supreme Court hearings take place on a tight schedule. They last only an hour or two. Each case is scheduled months in advance. This gives both sides time to prepare their cases, to write their briefs, and to gather any documents they believe support their arguments.[1]

The hearings are not like ordinary court trials. There are no witnesses and no jury. Attorneys do not bring evidence or exhibits with them. A Supreme Court case is pure argument, with both sides attempting to persuade the justices to favor their views of the Constitution and the law.

The nine justices give each side a chance to make its case—briefly. The justices may interrupt and question the attorneys at any time. They also may debate among themselves. Before the hearing, they have read many pages of legal briefs that lay out the case for each side. Finally, the chief justice brings down the gavel, and the proceedings end.

The case is not yet over. The justices may not agree on an opinion in the case. They may continue to debate the case for weeks and months. These proceedings take place behind closed doors. They can be long and bitter.[2]

The decision eventually arrives in the form of a written opinion. One justice has the responsibility of writing the opinion. Another justice, one who disagrees with the majority, writes a dissenting opinion (unanimous decisions are rare in Supreme Court cases). The opinions include the arguments and reasoning behind both sides of the questions. This process can take several months. When the Court issues its opinion, the case ends. There is no appeal.

Hearing the Case

The Court scheduled oral argument in *District of Columbia v. Heller* for March 18, 2008. Both sides had exactly one hour and fifteen minutes to argue their cases. As the petitioner, the District of Columbia had the opportunity to speak first. Walter Dellinger, representing D.C., rose to face the nine justices. Dellinger argued that the first clause of the Second Amendment reveals that the right to bear arms must be related to service in a public militia. The word "militia" in this amendment was synonymous with "people."

Chief Justice John Roberts and Justice Antonin Scalia challenged Dellinger. Why, asked Roberts, did the Second

Amendment state "the right of the people" if it meant "the right of militias"? Dellinger answered that "people" and "militia" meant the same. If, and only if, the government interfered with the forming of a militia, then it would be violating the Constitution.

The extent of the right, Dellinger declared, was the real issue in the case. The District of Columbia, like the states, had the authority to restrict weapons in the interest of public safety.

Justice Anthony Kennedy spoke of the rights of colonial settlers to own weapons in a dangerous environment.

In the spring of 1756, during the French and Indian War, a party of twenty Virginia militiamen led by Captain Jeremiah Smith fight off the invading French and their American Indian allies. Weapons were a necessity in colonial times, argued Justice Anthony Kennedy, but even then, there were rules in place governing gun ownership.

The Second Amendment gave the people a right to bear arms, because in the eighteenth century they were needed for defense not only against tyrants but also against criminals, American Indians, and wild animals. But Kennedy also pointed out that in the colonies, concealed weapons were banned, as was the carrying of arms in public places.

Dellinger also raised the legal status of the District of Columbia. Because it was not a state, the District of Columbia was not subject to the same constitutional restrictions as were the states. Nevertheless, allowing long guns meant that D.C. residents still enjoyed their constitutional right to "bear arms." Chief Justice Roberts answered: By this line of reasoning, the District of Columbia could ban books and allow newspapers and magazines and still uphold the First Amendment right to free expression.

Following Dellinger was the U.S. solicitor general, Paul Clement. His job was to present the position of the federal government on the case. Clement gave support to the individual-rights view of the Second Amendment. But he also defended federal gun laws. If the Supreme Court were to issue an opinion striking down all gun laws as unconstitutional, these federal laws would be challenged, and possibly overturned, in court. These included a federal law banning machine guns.

Although they were not invented until well after the Revolutionary War, machine guns are standard-issue weaponry for members of the armed forces as well as the National Guard. If all militia weapons are protected by the Second Amendment, therefore, ordinary citizens can buy and keep machine guns in their homes. Justice Scalia answered this point by stating that because machine guns were unknown to the framers of the Constitution, they could not be the intended subject of the Second Amendment. Therefore the Constitution does not protect a citizen's right to own one, and the government may regulate them.

Attorney Alan Gura, representing the respondent in the case, spoke for Richard Heller's right to own a handgun. Gura admitted that the Constitution allowed "reasonable" restrictions on firearms. This included the licensing and registration of handguns. But during the era of the Revolutionary War, the right to bear arms was equivalent to the right to self-defense. So a total ban on handguns went beyond reasonable. Instead, it represented the denial of a basic constitutional right.

Justice Stephen Breyer pointed out that in the early years of the United States, the government did indeed regulate firearms. The state of Massachusetts, as one example, banned citizens from keeping loaded weapons in their homes because of the risk of accidentally firing the weapons and causing injury, death, or a fire in the home: "So today, roughly, you can say no handguns in the city because of the risk of crime. Things change."[3] Breyer also suggested that judges should balance the interests of governments and private citizens when deciding whether Second Amendment rights are being violated.

After Gura spoke, Dellinger was given a short time

for a rebuttal (answer). The chief justice then brought down the gavel, and the court recessed. The argument had continued for a little over ninety minutes.[4] The case of *District of Columbia v. Heller* was one of the rare Supreme Court hearings that ran over its scheduled time. The justices would continue arguing the case, behind closed doors, for three months.

The Opinion Comes Down

On June 26, 2008, the Supreme Court announced its decision in the case of *District of Columbia v. Heller*. By a vote of 5–4, the court struck down the D.C. gun ban as a violation of the Second Amendment. Antonin Scalia, along with John Roberts, Clarence Thomas, Samuel Alito, and Anthony Kennedy, voted in the majority. Justices Ruth Bader Ginsburg, John Paul Stevens, David Souter, and Stephen Breyer voted to uphold the ban.

Justice Antonin Scalia wrote the majority opinion. Justices Thomas, Alito, Kennedy, and Roberts "joined" (also signed) the opinion. They stated that the Second Amendment protected a right of individual citizens and with the purpose to prevent the tyranny of kings and governments. The preface about militias describes only one such legitimate use of weapons by a citizen, but not all—implied also in the amendment was the right to bear arms for hunting and for defense of the home. For evidence, Scalia pointed to the Declaration of Rights passed by Pennsylvania in 1776.

However, the Second Amendment did not give a blanket right of all citizens to own any kind of weapon,

Justice Antonin Scalia wrote the majority opinion, which stated that the District of Columbia's Firearms Control Regulation Act was unconstitutional. He, along with John Roberts, Clarence Thomas, Samuel Alito, and Anthony Kennedy, believed private citizens had the right to own handguns to protect themselves.

and in any amount, they wished. Certain people could be barred from owning weapons, as well, and local governments had the right to ban weapons in public spaces, such as schools.

But the complete ban on handguns by the District of Columbia violated the Constitution. According to Scalia's opinion, it "amounts to a prohibition on an entire class of arms that Americans overwhelmingly choose for the lawful purpose of self-defense."[5] The meaning of "people" in the Second Amendment refers to individual citizens, as in the First Amendment and the Fourth Amendment. Further, forcing legal arms to be disassembled or disabled by a trigger lock prevents their lawful use for self-defense. For the first time in its history, the Supreme Court declared that individual self-defense was the basic right protected by the Second Amendment.

Scalia did not mention the special status of the District of Columbia in his opinion. By this, the majority confirmed the principle that the Constitution applies equally to residents of the District of Columbia as well as to the citizens of the fifty states.

However, the federal government did indeed have the right to limit the private ownership of machine guns, despite their common use in military service. This part of the opinion emphasizes the 1939 *Miller* decision: The government may not limit arms in "common use." Because machine guns were not in common use in James Madison's time, he could not have meant to protect them by the Second Amendment.

The majority opinion also knocked down Justice Breyer's suggestion of balancing public and private interest. By this view, no other basic constitutional right is subject to the "balancing of interests." Therefore, neither is the right to keep and to bear arms.

The Court ordered the District of Columbia to issue a license to Richard Heller to keep a handgun in his home. Because Heller and his attorneys had not brought up the subject of licensing, the Court did not give an opinion on the District of Columbia's right to register handguns. The constitutionality of gun registration, therefore, has not yet been decided by the Supreme Court.

The Dissent

Justice Stevens wrote a dissenting opinion, joined by justices Souter, Ginsburg, and Breyer. The Second Amendment did not mention specifically the right to use firearms for self-defense, as did important historical documents of the individual colonies. If Madison had meant to protect "self-defense," therefore, he would

Justice John Paul Stevens wrote the dissenting opinion, which upheld the D.C. handgun ban. He and Justices Ruth Bader Ginsburg, David Souter, and Stephen Breyer thought that the Second Amendment protected a well-regulated militia's right to bear arms, not the individual's, and that the District of Columbia had the power to regulate weapons in the name of public safety.

have included it in the Second Amendment. Instead, he prefaced the declaration of a right with a very different purpose: the arming of a well-regulated militia.

Stevens also pointed out that many lower courts had interpreted the Second Amendment to signify collective rather than individual rights. Further, the Court had found other federal and state firearms laws constitutional. This meant that the District of Columbia could regulate firearms if it chose to do so in the public interest.

He also mentioned the case of *United States v. Miller*, decided in 1939 on the meaning of the Second Amendment. In writing their opinions, the justices of the Supreme Court always look for precedent: previous decisions that touch on the same issues. Precedent is always a crucial part of their opinions. By tradition, the Court does not generally review or change a decision that it has already made, although it does sometimes return to previous decisions to clarify or to differ with them. Stevens saw the *Miller* decision as precedent for the *Heller* case, as *Miller* had made the difference between the military and nonmilitary use of weapons.

In a separate opinion, Justice Breyer repeated his support for the D.C. handgun ban. According to Breyer, the District of Columbia had made a permissible limitation on the right to own firearms, just as states and cities have always done. "There simply is no untouchable constitutional right guaranteed by the Second Amendment to keep loaded handguns in the house in crime-ridden urban areas," wrote Breyer.[6]

The justice also turned aside the evidence of rising crime statistics in the District of Columbia. Even though gun crimes had increased since the ban was passed, that did not mean the ban caused a rise in shootings and homicides. "As students of elementary logic know," Breyer wrote, "after it does not mean because of it. What would the District's crime rate have looked like without the ban? Higher? Lower? The same? Experts differ; and we, as judges, cannot say."[7] The Court's decision meant that local gun laws could, and would, be challenged and overturned—posing a danger to public safety in the cities plagued with gun violence.

Further, the "common use" argument mentioned by Scalia did not make sense. If there were no laws restricting machine guns, people might begin commonly using them to protect their homes. The Court would then have to find them constitutionally protected. The same principle might apply to tanks and heavy artillery. There had to be reasonable regulation of weapons by private citizens. States and cities had the right to carry out this regulation.

The fight over the Heller decision had just begun. Many legal scholars compared the decision to that in *Roe v. Wade,* the landmark Supreme Court case that struck down laws banning abortion. J. Harvie Wilkinson, a respected—and generally conservative—federal judge, wrote a scathing attack on the decision in the *Virginia Law Review,* entitled "Of Guns, Abortion, and the Unraveling of the Rule of Law."[8]

Wilkinson wrote that the Supreme Court decision resolved nothing and that it would only lead to more lawsuits. He saw the Supreme Court ignoring the history of the Constitution and the Second Amendment. The Court was also, in his view, advancing its own power over that of state and local lawmakers. As Wilkinson wrote: "Heller encourages Americans to do what conservative jurists warned for years they should not do: bypass the ballot and seek to press their political agenda in the courts."[9]

Several opponents responded with the point that the right to bear arms, unlike the right to an abortion, is given explicitly in the Constitution. They believed the court had made a correct interpretation of the Second Amendment. The analogy to *Roe v. Wade* may well be true, in that scholars and lawmakers will be arguing about *District of Columbia v. Heller* for a long time to come.

The Impact of the Decision

CHAPTER
7

Shortly after the decision in *District of Columbia v. Heller*, Richard Heller arrived at police headquarters in downtown D.C. He was carrying his .22 Colt revolver in a vinyl case. Reporters were there to greet him, to take photographs, and to ask questions.

Heller turned the gun over to a police clerk and began to fill out registration forms. The police took his fingerprints and gave Heller a paper with twenty questions. Heller's Colt was put through a ballistics test, then returned. If he wanted to carry it home, Heller had to keep the gun unloaded and the trigger locked.

The registration took about ninety minutes. The police would run a background check on Heller. This was still required by the Brady Bill, a federal law. A week later, Heller had his Colt registered. It was the first legal handgun in the hands of a private citizen in the District of Columbia since 1976.

The Impact of the Decision

In the wake of the decision, the District of Columbia went back to the drawing board. The District of Columbia passed the Firearms Control Emergency Act of 2008.[1] The new gun law replaced the law passed in 1976. The ordinance required gun owners to attend five hours of safety training in the use of firearms. All guns had to be registered and then registered again in three years.

Of course, many of these guns were already being kept, illegally, in homes of D.C. residents. In this case, the law granted a temporary amnesty. This amnesty lasted six months. It was not in force for gun owners who had committed a crime with their weapons.

Every six years, gun owners would have to go through a criminal background check. They also had to submit their legal guns to ballistics tests. This would help the police determine if the gun had been stolen or used in a crime.

The law passed as an emergency measure, good for ninety days. Gun owners had the right to register just

Richard Heller gives a thumbs up outside the Supreme Court after it ruled on June 26, 2008, that the Second Amendment protects the individual's right to keep guns in the home for self-defense. Attorney Clark Neily (right) helped bring into question the constitutionality of gun bans.

one weapon within that time. When the law expired, the District of Columbia passed another ordinance. The Second Firearms Control Emergency Amendment Act allowed some kinds of semiautomatic pistols. Automatic weapons, such as machine guns, were still illegal. Guns kept at home did not have to have trigger locks, if they were being used to defend against a legitimate threat. If there were children in the home, any gun had to be kept in a secure place.

Richard Heller was not through with the District of Columbia's gun laws. When he attempted to register a semiautomatic handgun, he was refused a license. He immediately challenged the new rules with a lawsuit. Heller and two other D.C. residents, Absalom Jordan and Amy McVey, claimed in federal court that the law violated their constitutional rights. Heller challenged the rules for registering guns, for passing background checks, for required ballistics test, and for keeping a gun loaded and ready to use.

Gun Battles

The Supreme Court decision overturned just one law: the District of Columbia's 1976 handgun ban. It did not declare an opinion on the right to carry concealed weapons, on gun-free zones, or on other gun laws in D.C. or other cities.

The gun-control debate, and the lawsuits, continued. For this reason, the decision came under criticism from both sides of the debate. "The decision is not a model of clarity," said Jon Vernick, a member of the Center for Gun Policy and Research, quoted in the *Chicago Tribune.* "There will be a bunch of lawsuits about a bunch of different kinds of federal, state, and local laws. It is a tragedy that resources that could be devoted to trying to prevent 30,000 gun-related deaths in the U.S. every year will instead be devoted to fighting lawsuits."[2]

Lawyers from the National Rifle Association went into action. The NRA was most active in northern Illinois. Their new cases would test handgun bans in Morton Grove, Oak Park, and Evanston, which bans handguns except for gun collectors and movie production companies. The NRA also sued the city of Chicago, where the law requires all guns to be registered and bans the registration of handguns.

The NRA based its lawsuits on the idea that the ruling in *District of Columbia v. Heller* applies not only to the District of Columbia but also to states and city governments. To support its argument, it cites the Fourteenth Amendment, which provides for "due process" for all persons within the United States.

The Battle of Morton Grove

Morton Grove, Illinois, is a small town of big importance in the gun-control debate. This community had banned all handguns in 1981, five years after the D.C. ban. It was the first city to follow the example of the District of Columbia. The ban drew wide interest from the press and the public.

The ban was immediately challenged in court. The case went to the Seventh Circuit Court of Appeals.

In December 1982, the court found the Second Amendment applied only to federal law. As precedent, it cited *Presser v. Illinois,* the nineteenth-century case that found the Second Amendment did not prevent the city of Chicago from banning a private militia.

Quite a bit of time had passed since *Presser v. Illinois.* Opponents of the gun ban believed the case was no longer "good law," meaning no longer valid. The Supreme Court had passed different opinions since then on the subject of the Fourteenth Amendment. By these decisions, the amendment implied that "due process" included the articles of the Bill of Rights. This meant that state and local laws also had to recognize and to abide by the Second Amendment.

The Supreme Court denied the petition to hear the Morton Grove case, however. The city's gun ban remained in effect until the decision in *District of Columbia v. Heller.* Not wanting to spend limited resources fighting the suits, Morton Grove and several other cities canceled their handgun bans immediately. Other cities with gun bans, including Chicago, prepared to fight the lawsuits.

Morton Grove kept bans on hand grenades, automatic rifles, BB guns, and some weapons used in the martial arts. In his written opinion, Justice Scalia had found that James Madison could not have had machine guns in mind when writing the Second Amendment. By this, Morton Grove sees, as do most other cities, machine guns as still not having constitutional protection.

Concealed Carry and the Gun-Free Zone

In Georgia, the General Assembly followed Florida's example, passing a law allowing "concealed carry" by those licensed to own handguns. The law specifically included public parks, restaurants, and nonsecure zones at Atlanta's busy Hartsfield Airport (a federal law bans guns in areas past security checkpoints). The management of the Atlanta airport immediately declared their property exempt from the new law.

Several members of Congress weighed in with their support. Arguing that concealed weapons pose a terrorism risk, they sought to extend control of nonsecure areas to the Transportation Security Administration (TSA), the federal agency that staffs checkpoints and guards secure zones, such as boarding gates and airport runways. If the issue goes to a federal court, Atlanta and other U.S. airports could, eventually, require security checks and metal detectors at their entrance doors.

Seeking another way around the Supreme Court decision, hundreds of cities passed ordinances establishing "gun-free zones." Federal laws on gun-free zones are already in effect throughout the country, including one law that bans guns within one thousand feet of any school. New laws also banned them in parks, enclosed public places, such as sports stadiums and shopping malls; bus and train terminals; public parking lots; and government offices.

Gun-rights advocates fought back, making the point

Gun-rights supporters hold up banners outside the Supreme Court after it ruled in their favor in the *District v. Heller* case.

that gun-free zones would do nothing to stop a criminal from bringing a weapon anywhere he or she wished. Erich Pratt, a member of Gun Owners of America, gave his stance to a newspaper reporter: "Declaring an area gun-free will not stop a criminal. . . . You've never seen them pick a police station to start shooting. They're going to pick an area where they can be the only one there with a gun."[3]

Cities passing new laws on handguns need to work around the Supreme Court decision in *District of Columbia v. Heller*. Many of these cities understand the decision to mean that only a complete ban on handguns, by law-abiding citizens, is contrary to the Second Amendment. Certain weapons can be banned, as can bringing weapons into certain places.

These cities also see the decision as applying only to the District of Columbia, which is still a federal zone that does not necessarily enjoy all the constitutional rights and authorities of the individual states. The law on banning gun ownership by convicted criminals and the mentally ill is supported by both sides in the gun-control debate.

Despite their victory in *District of Columbia v. Heller*, gun-rights supporters saw the victory of Democratic candidate Barack Obama as a serious setback to their cause. In the months after Obama took office as president, sales of guns and ammunition at shops and gun shows increased sharply. Many believed Obama's election would lead to new restrictions on the right to own and to carry a weapon and that the president's new appointments to the Supreme Court would allow gun-control advocates to bring the Second Amendment again under scrutiny.

In the meantime, a bloody turf war among drug-dealing gangs in northern Mexico brought U.S. gun-control laws into focus in late 2008. With guns strictly controlled in Mexico, and automatic weapons banned even for use by the police, many of the gangs were obtaining their weapons through "straw buyers" north of the border. These buyers legally purchased weapons in U.S. gun shops and at gun shows, concealed them in vehicles, then transported them across the border to Mexico. Gun dealers and smugglers benefited from lax enforcement by police, customs officers, and border patrol agents and from corruption among Mexican police, some of whom were accepting bribes to ignore the illegal gun trafficking.

The continuing debate over gun control makes it likely that the Second Amendment will come under Supreme Court review again. The constitutionality of many gun-control laws has not been decided. Defense lawyers are still bringing their appeals to state and federal courts. The NRA, the Cato Institute, and other organizations are working to convince the public of their points of view. Skilled lawyers stand ready to test their cases, if necessary, all the way to the highest court in the land.

1689—The English Parliament passes a Bill of Rights, which establishes the right of Protestants "suitable to their condition" to have firearms for defensive purposes.

1787—James Madison completes the final draft of the Bill of Rights, the first ten amendments to the Constitution, in which the Second Amendment guarantees the right to "bear arms."

1886—In the case of *Presser v. Illinois,* the Supreme Court finds that the states have the constitutional authority to regulate militias.

1934—The U.S. Congress passes the National Firearms Act, a federal law controlling ownership of guns. The law requires registration of certain weapons.

1939—In the case of *United States v. Miller,* the Supreme Court upholds the National Firearms Act and finds the regulation of certain firearms constitutional.

1968—By the federal Gun Control Act, certain handguns are banned.

1976—The District of Columbia passes the Firearms Control Regulation Act, effectively banning the ownership of handguns by private citizens.

1993—Congress passes the Brady Handgun Violence Protection Act, also known as the Brady Bill, which requires background checks and waiting periods for purchases of firearms.

2002—*Parker v. District of Columbia* is filed in a federal appeals court.

2005—President George W. Bush appoints John Roberts and Samuel Alito to the Supreme Court.

2007—The case of *District of Columbia v. Heller* is decided in favor of the plaintiffs. The District of Columbia appeals the decision to the Supreme Court, which grants the petition for a hearing.

2008—On March 18, the Supreme Court hears oral argument in the case of *District of Columbia v. Heller.* On June 26, the Court announces its finding for the respondent, Richard Heller, and strikes down the D.C. gun ban.

Chapter Notes

INTRODUCTION

1. Thomas Streissguth, *Eyewitness History: The Roaring Twenties*, rev. ed. (New York: Facts On File, 2007), pp. 298–299.
2. "National Firearms Act," *ATF Online—Bureau of Alcohol, Tobacco, Firearms and Explosives*, August 25, 1998, < http://www.atf.gov/pub/fire-explo_pub/nfa.htm > (August 4, 2009).
3. Bryan Frye, "The Peculiar Story of *U.S. v. Miller*," *NYU Journal of Law and Liberty*, March 1, 2008, p. 59.
4. "Amendment 2—Right to Bear Arms," *U.S. Constitution Online*, February 6, 2009, < http://www.usconstitution.net/const.html > (August 4, 2009).
5. Frye, p. 67.
6. *United States v. Miller*, 307 U.S. 174 (1939), *FindLaw.com*, 2009, < http://caselaw.lp.findlaw.com/scripts/getcase.pl?navby = CASE&court = US&vol = 307&page = 174 > (August 4, 2009).

CHAPTER 1. Trouble in the District of Columbia

1. "Gun Control Act of 1968, Public Law 90–618," *ATF Online—Bureau of Alcohol, Tobacco, Firearms and Explosives*, n.d., < http://www.atf.gov/pub/fire-explo_pub/gca.htm > (August 4, 2009).
2. "Brady Handgun Violence Prevention Act," *Carnegie Mellon School of Computer Science*, n.d., < http://www.cs.cmu.edu/afs/cs/usr/wbardwel/public/nfalist/brady_act.txt > (August 4, 2009).
3. "About the Brady Campaign," *Brady Campaign to Prevent Gun Violence*, 2009, < http://www.bradycampaign.org/about/ > (August 4, 2009).
4. "Mission Statement," *Second Amendment Foundation Online*, 2009, < http://www.saf.org/default.asp?p = mission > (August 4, 2009).
5. "District of Columbia Crime Rates, 1960–2007," *Disaster Center*, 2008, < http://www.disastercenter.com/crime/dccrime.htm > (August 4, 2009).

6. W. Caffrey, "Do You Have a Right to Police Protection?" *Taking on Gun Control,* May 12, 2000, < http://hematite.com/dragon/policeprot.html > (August 4, 2009).
7. "District of Columbia Crime Rates, 1960–2007."
8. Martha Brant and Stuart Taylor, Jr., "A New Shot at History," *Newsweek,* December 3, 2007, < http://www.newsweek.com/id/72034 > (August 4, 2009).
9. "A Brief Overview of the Supreme Court," *Supreme Court of the United States,* n.d., < http://www.supremecourtus.gov/about/briefoverview.pdf > (August 4, 2009).

CHAPTER 2. The Road to the Supreme Court

1. John E. Kramer, "About IJ: IJ's Merry Band of Litigators," *Institute for Justice,* 2009, < http://ij.org/index.php?option = com_content&task = view&id = 550&Itemid = 223 > (August 4, 2009).
2. "About Cato," *Cato Institute,* n.d., < http://www.cato.org/about.php > (August 4, 2009).
3. "U.S. Constitution: Fourteenth Amendment," *FindLaw.com,* 2009, < http://caselaw.lp.findlaw.com/data/constitution/amendment14/ > (August 4, 2009).
4. Martha Brant and Stuart Taylor, Jr., "A New Shot at History," *Newsweek,* December 3, 2007, < http://www.newsweek.com/id/72034 > (August 4, 2009).
5. John Fund, "Defense Bill," *Wall Street Journal,* September 27, 2007, < http://www.opinionjournal.com/diary/?id = 110005678 > (August 4, 2009).
6. "U.S. District Court Memorandum Opinion in *Seegars v. Ashcroft,*" *Violence Policy Center,* January 14, 2004, < http://www.vpc.org/graphics/SeegarsOpinion.pdf > (August 4, 2009).

CHAPTER 3. The Context of the Constitution

1. Carl T. Bogus, et al., Amicus Curiae Brief in Support of Petitioners, *District of Columbia v. Heller,* Supreme Court 07-290, p. 6.

2. Don B. Kates, "Handgun Prohibition and the Original Meaning of the Second Amendment," *Michigan Law Review,* vol. 82 (1983), pp. 204–273, *GunCite,* June 29, 2008, < http://www. guncite.com/journals/kmich.html > (August 4, 2009).

3. "Declaration of the Causes and Necessity of Taking Up Arms (July 6, 1775)," *National Center for Public Policy Research,* 2009, < http://www.nationalcenter.org/1775DeclarationofArms. html > (August 4, 2009).

4. Earl Kruschke, *Gun Control: A Reference Handbook* (Santa Barbara, Calif.: ABC-CLIO, 1995), p. 74.

5. Bogus et al., p. 10.

6. "U.S. Constitution: Article I," *FindLaw.com,* 2009, < http:// caselaw.lp.findlaw.com/data/constitution/article01/ > (August 4, 2009).

7. "Alexander J. Dallas' Notes of the Pennsylvania Ratification Convention P.M. (December 12, 1787)," *The Constitutional Source Project,* n.d., < http://www.consource.org/index.asp? bid = 582&documentid = 2051 > (September 1, 2009).

CHAPTER 4. The Original Intent:
Individual v. Collective Rights

1. *Presser v. State of Illinois,* 116 U.S. 252 (1886), *FindLaw. com,* 2009, < http://caselaw.lp.findlaw.com/scripts/getcase. pl?court = US&vol = 116&invol = 252 > (August 4, 2009).

2. Don B. Kates, "Handgun Prohibition and the Original Meaning of the Second Amendment," *Michigan Law Review,* vol. 82 (1983), p. 204, *GunCite,* June 29, 2008, < http://www.guncite. com/journals/kmich.html > (August 4, 2009).

3. *United States v. Emerson,* No. 99-10331 (5th Circuit Ct. 2001), *FindLaw.com,* 2009, < http://caselaw.lp.findlaw.com/cgi-bin/ getcase.pl?court = 5th&navby = docket&no = 9910331cr0 > (August 4, 2009).

4. Brian Doherty, "How the Second Amendment Was Restored: The Inside Story of How a Gang of Libertarian Lawyers Made Constitutional History," *Reason Online,* December 2008, < http:// www.reason.com/news/show/129991.html > (August 4, 2009).

5. Quoted by Glenn Harlan Reynolds, "A Critical Guide to the Second Amendment," *Tennessee Law Review*, vol. 62, 1995, p. 461, *GunCite*, June 29, 2008, < http://www.guncite.com/journals/reycrit.html#fn28 > (August 4, 2009).

CHAPTER 5. The Politics of a Decision

1. "Common Legal Challenges to Laws Banning Assault Weapons," *Legal Community Against Violence*, 2004, < http://www.lcav.org/library/reports_analyses/Banning_Assault_Weapons_A_Legal_Primer_8.05_Appendix_D.pdf > (August 4, 2009).
2. "Gun Control Advocates Hate Alito Nomination," *About.com*, November 2, 2005, < http://usgovinfo.about.com/b/2005/11/02/gun-control-advocates-hate-alito-nomination.htm > (January 3, 2009).
3. Senator Patrick Leahy, quoted in "Leahy: Alito a Threat to Our Fundamental Rights," *Truthout.org*, January 24, 2006, < http://www.truthout.org/article/leahy-alito-a-threat-our-fundamental-rights > (August 5, 2009).
4. Jennifer Steinhauer, "At State Level, More Attempts to Limit Guns," *New York Times*, April 15, 2008, < http://www.nytimes.com/2008/04/15/us/15guns.html > (August 5, 2009).
5. Nicholas Wapshott, "Disney Under Fire," *New Statesman*, July 31, 2008, < http://www.newstatesman.com/society/2008/07/disney-work-company-bringing > (August 5, 2009).

CHAPTER 6. The Court Decides

1. "U.S. Supreme Court Procedures," *U.S. Courts*, n.d., < http://www.uscourts.gov/outreach/topics/hamdan/procedures.html > (August 5, 2009).
2. Jeffrey Toobin, *The Nine: Inside the Secret World of the Supreme Court* (New York: Anchor Books, 2008).
3. Linda Greenhouse, "Court Weighs Right to Guns, and Its Limits," *New York Times*, March 19, 2008, < http://www.nytimes.com/2008/03/19/washington/19scotus.html > (August 5, 2009).
4. Transcript of the oral argument in *District of Columbia v. Heller*, 478 F. 3d 370 (2008), *Supreme Court of the United States*,

March 18, 2008, < http://www.supremecourtus.gov/oral_arguments/argument_transcripts/07-290.pdf > (August 5, 2009).

5. Written opinion in *District of Columbia v. Heller*, 478 F. 3d 370 (2008), *SCOTUS Wiki*, August 27, 2008, < http://www.scotuswiki.com/index.php?title = DC_v._Heller > (August 5, 2009), along with all the submitted briefs, a transcript of the oral argument, press clips, a blog, and analysis of the case. The *SCOTUS (Supreme Court of the United States) Wiki* offers access to every document in the court file.

6. Ibid.

7. Ibid.

8. J. Harvie Wilkinson III, "Of Guns, Abortion, and the Unraveling of the Rule of Law," *Virginia Law Review*, vol. 95, no. 2, p. 253, last revised May 2, 2009, < http://papers.ssrn.com/sol3/papers.cfm?abstract_id = 1265118 > (August 5, 2009).

9. Ibid.

CHAPTER 7. The Impact of the Decision

1. "Mayor Fenty, Council Unveil Firearms Legislation and Regulations," *District of Columbia*, July 14, 2008, < http://www.dc.gov/mayor/news/release.asp?id = 1333 > (August 5, 2009).

2. Dahleen Glanton, "New Battles Erupt Over Gun Laws," *Chicago Tribune*, July 27, 2008, < http://archives.chicagotribune.com/2008/jul/27/nation/chi-gunlaws_bdjul27 > (August 5, 2009).

3. Ibid.

Glossary

Bill of Rights—The first ten amendments to the U.S. Constitution; named after a document passed in England in 1689.

Brady Handgun Violence Protection Act—A federal law that requires background checks and a waiting period for all gun purchases.

brief—An essay arguing legal points for one side of a court case.

Cato Institute—A "think tank" that largely supports conservative views on politics, economic matters, and law.

collective rights model—That view of the Second Amendment that sees the right to bear arms as depending on an individual's militia service.

dissent—An opinion contrary to the majority position taken by a court.

Firearms Control Emergency Act of 2008—An ordinance passed by Washington, D.C., after its handgun ban was struck down by the Supreme Court.

Firearms Control Regulation Act of 1976—An ordinance passed by Washington, D.C., which bans the possession of handguns within the city.

Gun Control Act of 1968—A federal law that was passed to ban the sale of cheap handguns.

Handgun Control, Inc.—An organization that advocates for stricter and more uniform gun laws.

hearing—A court session in which both sides may present evidence and witnesses, explain their positions, and debate the law.

individual rights model—The view of the Second Amendment that sees the right to bear arms as belonging to individuals, and not necessarily in the context of militia service.

Institute for Justice—A libertarian "think tank" that argues for limited government and constitutional rights according to the original intent of the framers of the U.S. Constitution.

join—In appeals court practice, to add one's name to a written opinion.

militia—A company of civilian volunteers organized for the common defense.

National Firearms Act—A law passed in 1934 that required owners of certain types of weapons to register them and to pay a tax.

National Rifle Association—An organization that advocates for stricter enforcement of existing gun laws and argues against new legal restrictions on gun ownership.

opinion—A written declaration from a court, summarizing the arguments of both sides of the case and giving the reason for the court's decision.

remand—To send a case back to a lower court with instructions on how to proceed.

Standard Model—The interpretation of the Second Amendment that supports the individual's right to bear arms, and one not dependent on militia service.

stay—An order temporarily halting all proceedings in a court trial.

writ of certiorari—A document issued by a higher court allowing a hearing and review of a lower-court decision.

Further Reading

Cornell, Saul. *A Well-Regulated Militia: The Founding Fathers and the Origins of Gun Control in America*. New York: Oxford University Press, 2008.

Doherty, Brian. *Gun Control on Trial: Inside the Supreme Court Battle Over the Second Amendment*. Washington, D.C.: The Cato Institute, 2008.

Halbrook, Stephen P. *The Founders' Second Amendment: Origins of the Right to Bear Arms*. Chicago: Ivan R. Dee, 2008.

Korwin, Alan. *The Heller Case: Gun Rights Affirmed*. Scottsdale, Ariz.: Bloomfield Press, 2008.

Roleff, Tamara. *Gun Control: Opposing Viewpoints*. Detroit, Mich.: Greenhaven Press, 2007.

Young, David. *The Founders' View of the Right to Bear Arms: A Definitive History of the Second Amendment*. Ontonagon, Mich.: Golden Oak Books, 2007.

Internet Addresses

"District of Columbia v. Heller,"
   Oyez: Supreme Court Media
   http://www.oyez.org/cases/2000-2009/2007/
      2007_07_290/

"District of Columbia v. Heller,"
   Cornell University Law School
   http://www.law.cornell.edu/supct/html/07-290.
      ZS.html

"District of Columbia v. Heller," SCOTUS (Supreme
   Court of the United States) Wiki
   http://www.scotuswiki.com/index.php?title=
      DC_v._Heller

Index

Index